The Landlord's Troubleshooter

Robert Irwin

Happy Birthday !
Keep Smiling !!
Mom
July 7 - 94

**Real Estate
Education Company**
a division of Dearborn Financial Publishing, Inc.

While a great deal of care has been taken to provide accurate and current information, the ideas, suggestions, general principles and conclusions presented in this text are subject to local, state and federal laws and regulations, court cases and any revisions of same. The reader is thus urged to consult legal counsel regarding any points of law—this publication should not be used as a substitute for competent legal advice.

Publisher: Kathleen A. Welton
Acquisitions Editor: Patrick J. Hogan
Associate Editor: Karen A. Christensen
Senior Project Editor: Jack L. Kiburz
Editorial Assistant: Kristen G. Landreth
Interior Design: Lucy Jenkins
Cover Design: Salvatore Concialdi

© 1994 by Dearborn Financial Publishing, Inc.

Published by Real Estate Education Company,
a division of Dearborn Financial Publishing, Inc.

Printed in the United States of America

94 95 96 10 9 8 7 6 5 4 3 2 1

·

Library of Congress Cataloging-in-Publication Data

Irwin, Robert, 1941–
    The Landlord's troubleshooter / by Robert Irwin.
      p. cm.
    Includes index.
    ISBN 0-7931-0954-X
    1. Real estate management. 2. Rental housing—Management.
3. Landlord and tenant. I. Title.
HD1394.I78   1994
333.5′4—dc20   94-7177
                                                                  CIP

Contents

PART THREE   Moving Tenants Out

PART FIVE   Resources

Preface

◆◆◆◆◆◆◆

Most landlords and landladies I know who have troubles want answers—and quick—to questions that are sometimes very tricky. How do you get the rent when tenants are late? What do you do about a tenant who paints the apartment purple? What happens when the market is terrible and you can't get the unit rented? How do you get rid of a tenant who won't pay, and do so more quickly and cheaply than resorting to eviction?

I appreciate these questions and hundreds like them because I've been a landlord most of my life. I started managing property when I was 18, and that was more than three decades ago. I've been a landlord more or less continually ever since. While I wouldn't want to say that I've run into every possible situation a landlord can face, I've probably run into most of them. And I've worked with, and drawn on the experience of, some very excellent property manager friends and professionals who have run into nearly all the rest of the problems.

Thus, when I began getting calls from friends, many of whom were new to managing property, asking how to handle this situation or that, it seemed only natural to come up with a book of landlords' answers for landlords' questions.

The Landlord's Troubleshooter is for everyone from casual landlords and landladies (i.e., you just have one house or condo that you perhaps fell into and must rent out) to investors who buy large apartment buildings.

Regardless of how many or how few your rental units, the questions are frequently the same. And so are the right answers.

It's important to understand at the outset, however, that I don't intend this book to be a course on how to become a landlord, such as you might take at night school. I don't have the patience to write that sort of thing, and I certainly know I wouldn't have the patience to read it.

Rather, this book is intended as a quick and easy problem solver. I don't expect you to start at page one and read through to the end (although you certainly may, if you wish). My hope is that when you are in the midst of renting property and suddenly have an urgent problem or need, you will come here and be able to quickly find a good, practical solution.

I've organized this book under four broad headings: (1) common landlord gripes and remedies, (2) getting and keeping better tenants, (3) getting rid of undesirable tenants and (4) handling your rental as a business proposition. Whether you're just an inadvertent landlord (you couldn't sell your home and now you have to rent it out) or a pro, you should be able to quickly locate the answers you need.

Of course, I'm not saying you're going to like all the answers I suggest (such as bribing a bad tenant to leave or personally walking through and inspecting the property with tenants before they move in and after they move out). But I have found that these answers work for me and many excellent professional residential property managers as well.

My goal was to create a solutions book. When you're a landlord or landlady and you've got a problem you can't figure out, you need a source where you can find a quick and practical answer that gets results. And perhaps even more important, you need to learn how to avoid such problems in the future.

This is that practical book. If you're a landlord or landlady and are out there in the rental battlefields, it is your defense weapon. Use it to protect yourself, and come out a winner.

PART ONE

Common Landlord Gripes and Remedies

1

When the Rent Is Late

Every landlord sooner or later experiences late rent payments. If you're reading this chapter now, perhaps you're currently having this problem and are looking for a solution. If so, let's clearly define what you are worried about.

What Late Rent Means to the Landlord

There are really three worries that most landlords have when the rent is late (and the tenant has not called to explain):

1. Will it cause me to miss my own payments for mortgage, insurance, utilities or other?

2. Does the late rent portend more serious trouble to come in the future? (Will this rent be late again next month and the month after? Is the tenant going to refuse to pay altogether and thus cause me real grief?)

3. Assuming it's the first late rent payment from a good payer, how do I handle this without offending and potentially losing the good tenant?

It's important to understand that when the rent is late, most land-lords—particularly those new to the game—experience two emotions: fear and anger. You're afraid because the late rent threatens your own-ership of the property. In most cases landlords have a very thin margin. You probably are counting on that rent to make a hefty mortgage payment. Without the rent, you'll have to come up with the money elsewhere, and that can cause you serious difficulty. And you're angry at the tenant for putting you in this position.

What's important to remember is that the tenant is also probably experiencing fear and anger. The tenant may be afraid of what will happen because of the late rent. In the case of most tenants (we'll talk about problems with "professional tenants" later), they don't know what you can or will do. They're worried about their credit standing and the roof over their heads. And they are often angry at themselves (though this can quickly be redirected at you) for letting this situation occur.

If you allow your emotions to rule and respond in a fearful or angry way, chances are you will provoke a similar response from the tenant. You could actually turn a harmless situation of a payment lost in the mail into a serious problem that can mean really late rent, a lost tenant or worse.

◆────────────────────────────────

Landlord's Quiz

What's worse than a tenant who moves without paying?
You're a new landlord if you ask that. The answer: A tenant who stays and won't pay!

────────────────────────────────

The Way To Proceed

It's important at the onset to control your emotions. If the rent is late, it's a business problem and needs to be dealt with accordingly. You should proceed in the following manner.

Define the Problem

Before taking any action you must determine why the rent is late. There are many, many reasons, from the simple and innocuous to the difficult and underhanded. You can't know what to do until you figure out what the problem really is. In case you're scratching your head trying to figure it out, here's a list of some possible causes for late rent:

Easy Problems

- It's in the mail. (Yes, once in a great while a rent check really does get lost in the mail—though not too often!)

- The tenant forgot. (Incredible, isn't it? How can anyone forget to pay the rent? But it happens.)

- There's a problem with the house, and the tenant is purposely holding back the rent until you fix it. (You should know about this already from earlier conversations with the tenant.)

- The tenants don't have the money because a check they are expecting is late. (That's their problem, right? Except now they're making it yours.)

- The tenant lost his or her job and just doesn't have the money. (This is happening more and more in today's economy. The trouble is, now you have to do something about it.)

- The tenant is sick, can't work and can't even get out of bed to call you. (It helps if you're a doctor. If not, you could have a problem.)

- The tenant won't pay and won't give a reason. (You have a serious problem.)

Difficult Problems.   How do you know if the problem is easy or difficult? You talk to the tenant. You can never define the problem yourself and can only figure it out through communication.

◆

Landlord's Quiz

What's a landlord in who never goes out to talk to his or her tenants? The answer? In foreclosure!

When the rent is late, I always make it a point to drop by to see the tenant. If it's a tenant who has previously paid well and who pays through the mail, I might wait as long as three days before dropping by. For a really good tenant, I might just call up and say, "By the way, the rent payment hasn't arrived. Is there a problem?" This tenant will probably be surprised, will say he or she mailed the check a week ago and will be happy to cancel the check and give me a cashier's check or even cash if I want it. I then drop by and pick up the rent. There are no hard feelings. I haven't lost a good tenant. And my worries are assuaged.

◆

When Late Rent Is Okay

Sometimes you just have to accept late rent. I once had a tenant who depended on her Social Security check to pay the rent. She was always five days late. The reason? Her Social Security check arrived on the fifth of the month.

I had a choice. I could rant and rave and demand that payment be made on the first, in which case it would still arrive on the fifth. Or I could accept the fact that she would always be punctually five days late. She was a good tenant, always paid late promptly and I never said a word. She stayed for nearly seven years and never complained about anything, even once. She was one of the best tenants I ever had.

Locate the Tenant

Therefore, when the rent is late, your first task is to find the tenant and determine why. Why is the rent late, and what does the tenant intend to do about it?

Finding the tenant is usually easy. When I'm looking, I just come by at dinnertime. Most tenants are home then. Sometimes, however, the tenant isn't home. They aren't home when you come by at dinnertime, in the morning or in the afternoon. You may come back several times and the tenant still isn't around. It's easy to become aggravated, frustrated or even hostile and lose your perspective. Now, even if it's all innocent, you can begin to see a plot and overreact.

Who knows? It could have been a family emergency—perhaps a son or daughter was injured in an auto accident or a distant parent fell desperately ill. In such times most of us forget mundane things like rent and just react to the immediate need.

What should you do? If you've got a good rental agreement and application (see Chapter 9 and Appendix A), they will list a few phone numbers of relatives. Give them a call. After all, you have a legitimate concern—your rent. Find out if something happened in the family. If it is an emergency and it's a good tenant, be especially nice. Let the person you call know you're concerned. Ask them to have the tenant call you, and let them know that if they need time, you'll work something out. Chances are good that you'll get a call back within a few hours and a rent check the next day.

If the phone calls to relatives don't work, it's time to become a snoop. Go around and talk to the neighbors. It's positively amazing what neighbors know. Tell the neighbors you own the property, you can't find the tenants and you're worried that something might be amiss. If the neighbors know anything, they'll dump it right on you. Rather than an emergency, there may be marital troubles. Perhaps there was a terrible fight and they split—the husband in one direction and the wife in another. Or the tenant got laid off from work and just packed up and took off someplace else.

◆──

When Abandonment Is the Best Kind of Termination

I had a very good tenant who stayed in my property for over two years. Then one day the rent was late. I called, but there was no answer. I came by and the front door was locked up and nobody was home. I talked to the neighbors and they said that the night before my tenants had packed up their belongings in a rental truck and left.

I rechecked the property and found the back door unlocked and the house dirty but empty. They had abandoned it.

I was perfectly happy. They hadn't cost me any lost rent. I still had the security deposit to take care of cleaning, and I could reclaim my house. Yes, I would have preferred a more orderly termination, but given the alternative of what they could have done (i.e., stayed, not paid and ruined the house), I was thrilled.

In a worst-case scenario where you can't find the tenants and the relatives and neighbors aren't helpful, leave a card on the front door saying you were there and will return. Hopefully, sooner or later they will turn up. If they don't, you may have to start eviction action (see Chapter 16), but that's particularly hard if the tenants simply aren't there.

But take heart; in 30 years of being a landlord only once did my tenants leave all their furniture and disappear, and that was a long time ago. Most tenants are usually still there, even if they're just hiding out and pretending not to be home.

Listen to the Tenant

Remember, your first goal is to find out why the rent is late. Only after you've found out what the problem is can you take appropriate action. You're there first and foremost to listen.

Landlord's Rule #1

Go into the corner and say three times, "I will do *nothing* until I hear what the tenant has to say."

Other Issues

Okay, the rent is late, you've found the tenant and you've listened. Now what? Assuming the problem isn't something simple like the rent is lost in the mail, you now have to decide on a course of action.

We'll discuss what action you should take in Chapter 2. But first we'll discuss a few side issues to help you ensure that the rent isn't late in the future.

Mailing versus Picking Up the Rent

Should you have the tenant mail the check to you or go out and pick it up personally? The answer, of course, depends entirely on the tenant. In my experience I have found that most often tenants in low-cost properties expect the landlord to come by on rent day and collect payment. If you don't come by, they don't pay.

Middle-cost to upper-cost properties, on the other hand, often attract tenants who would think you absurd (if not a little paranoid) if you came by to collect the rent monthly. They assume they will send it in along with the utility, phone and other bills.

I have done it both ways and can assure you that getting the rent check in the mail is by far the easier method, when it arrives. But in either case, if the rent is late, you must make a personal appearance and do so quickly.

If you are having the rent sent to you, one technique that some landlords use successfully is to mail the tenant a postage-paid envelope around the middle of the month. All the tenant has to do is put the check in the envelope and drop it in the mailbox. This simple device is quite inexpensive and can save a lot of late payments.

Landlord's Rule #2 _____

Never own rental property in an area in which you are personally afraid to go and pick up the rent.

If the Check Bounces

Sometimes the rent check will bounce. Either it's the regular rent check sent in the mail or the check you get when you show up in person to collect on late rent. What do you do?

The answer is that from then on with that tenant you avoid personal checks and get cash, a cashier's check or a money order instead. You simply have to say you can't be bothered with the delays and inconvenience of bounced checks. If the tenant wants to continue as such, he or she must pay in cash or cash equivalent.

In addition, I deposit any rent check that I get in the mail *immediately*, the same day if possible. I also have an arrangement with my bank (and you can have a similar one with yours) in which any check that doesn't clear results in an immediate phone call to notify me of the problem. I don't wait the three to five days it takes for the bank to send out a letter. Thus, I usually know within two days when a rent check doesn't clear the tenant's bank. What do I do then?

I go down to my bank and pick up the check, which usually has a stamp on the back that says it wasn't paid because of insufficient funds. I then take the check and go see the tenant.

I inform the tenant that not only is the rent late, but now I've been given a bad check. The criminal penalties for issuing a bad check vary from one area of the country to another but are getting increasingly more severe. I know what the penalties are in my area, and I mention them.

I am willing to accept payment in cash in exchange for a bad check. I will also take a money order and, if they are legitimate, traveler's checks. I will not take another personal check, although I will accept a cashier's check. (*Note:* Within the last few years banks have sometimes weaseled out of honoring cashier's checks, sometimes even their own, depending on the circumstances.)

If the tenant cannot or will not give me cash or cash equivalent for the bad check, I serve the first eviction notice. I also hang onto the bad check; it can prove helpful if the matter ever gets to a court hearing.

Caution! Beware of Partial Rents

Many times a tenant will say that they can't pay the entire month's rent but can pay for a week or two weeks. They'll give you the two weeks and pay the remainder at the end of that time.

Most landlords feel that one in the hand is worth 12 in the bush when it comes to rent. It's better to take the two weeks and worry about the rest later.

But I say yes and no. If it's a good tenant in a bad spot who needs just a little help, you're probably safe in taking the partial rent. However, an unscrupulous tenant can now say that by accepting part payment, you've changed the terms of the rental arrangement. It's now a weekly rental instead of a monthly rental. (Many areas have very different laws regulating weekly rentals.)

Furthermore, if you serve an eviction notice (the first one) and then accept a partial rent payment, you have in effect called off the eviction proceedings. If the tenant subsequently doesn't pay anymore, in most locales you must start all over again with that first notice. This can cause you to lose many weeks of your most precious asset—time.

The Bottom Line

Don't ever let late rent slip by. The rent is your due for providing housing to the tenant. Every day that it goes unpaid means that you are providing free housing. Furthermore, unpaid rent means that your financial security and even ownership of your property are being threatened.

2

•••◆•••

When the Tenant
Doesn't Pay Up

The rent is late; you've gone out to see the tenants. You still don't have the money. Now what do you do?

In Chapter 1 we talked about the easy solution. The rent was lost in the mail, so you simply ask for and get cash or cash equivalent. Now the problem is more difficult.

◆

Argument Ender

If the tenant continues to insist the check was lost in the mail, don't argue. Just agree and say you want another check—a cashier's check this time—or cash, immediately. The lost check can be cancelled, or you'll return it whenever it shows up. That should end that line of argument by the tenant.

When the Tenant "Can't" Pay

The most common reason that a tenant will give for not paying the rent (after you've cleared up the business about it being lost in the mail) is that they don't have the money right now. There's been an unfortunate delay. The tenant's boss didn't get the paychecks out that week, or the money they were expecting from Aunt Bertha simply hasn't shown up. The tenant wants to pay but explains that they simply can't right now. If you're just willing to wait awhile—a few days, perhaps a week or two—they'll get the money to you.

Should you wait? No one wants to be unkind, but it's important to remember that renting property is a business just like any other. How long do you think a gas station owner, for example, can stay in business if he or she gives out free gas to everyone who stops by and says their tank is empty and they don't have any money?

These tenants obviously have a problem, but it's important to see just what they want to do with it: they want to take their problem and make it yours. Their problem is that they can't pay the rent right now, so it's their responsibility to find a solution. That solution must be that they either get the money from somewhere or they move out. If, however, you agree to allow them not to pay even for a short while (such as a week or two), now it's your problem. You have a nonpaying tenant. What are you going to do about it?

◆

Landlord's Quiz:

What is the only acceptable answer a tenant can give for late rent? Answer: "Sorry I'm late. Here's the rent, in cash."

Demanding the Rent

Don't let the tenant put you off. Experienced landlords know that in almost all cases tenants can come up with the money if they feel they have to. People usually have money in a savings account, or they can borrow it from relatives. But they hesitate to get it from such a source unless it's an emergency. And often they don't define late rent as an emergency.

It's important that rent be defined as a high-priority item. The rent must be paid first; otherwise, it can be put off to the end of a long list of other bills. You can be sympathetic, but you must make it clear that the rent must be paid, and on time. Perhaps you might say something such as, "I'm sorry to hear that. . . . (fill in the blank with the tenant's problem); but as you must know, the rent comes first. You have to have a roof over your head. I've made a special trip to collect it. I'm here for the rent, right now."

Once you make it clear that you are there for the rent and will not be moved until it's paid, the tenant will often come up with it. They will also learn that you are someone who stands up for himself or herself, and they will think twice the next month about putting you at the end of their list of people to be paid.

Demand the rent to which you are entitled, and you will get it—most of the time.

Landlord's Rule #3

Be a "no nonsense" landlord, but do *not* be mean, vindictive, loud, insulting or overbearing. Always speak quietly and calmly, but firmly. The rent is due. You're there to pick it up. There are no excuses.

The Tenant Won't Pay

On the other hand, the tenant simply may not be able or willing to pay. You must dig deeper to find out why. Is the breadwinner out of work? Was there an emergency (e.g., someone got into a car accident)? Did the money get spent elsewhere? Is the rent simply too high?

It may be time to reason with the tenant. If the rent is simply too high or they are in an impossible financial situation, you may want to suggest that the tenant consider moving to a lower-cost rental or even to a relative's home until things get better. You can point out that this will save the tenant's credit reputation and will convert them from being in an impossible rental situation to one that they can handle. You may even want to use some of their security deposit to facilitate this move. Remember, getting rid of a tenant who can't pay quickly is far better than having them stay while you try to collect rent in court.

I have even chipped in to help pay for movers to get a tenant who couldn't pay out of the property. Remember, you can't squeeze blood from a turnip or get water out of a stone. If they just don't have the money, then your best solution is to find an amicable way for them to move somewhere else.

On the other hand, if the excuse is implausible or they are adamant about staying or they refuse to work with you, you're probably in a situation that's only going to get worse. You will undoubtedly be best off to serve the tenant with the first eviction notice right on the spot. (See Chapter 16 on evictions.)

Sometimes serving an eviction notice results in your getting your rent paid if not immediately, within a day or two. If this tenant does pay up, however, make it perfectly clear to them that in the future you expect the rent to continue to be paid on time, or else that eviction notice will be back.

◆ Landlord's Dilemma

You want to keep the tenants, so you're afraid to begin eviction for fear of offending them. It's true that you could lose a tenant by serving the first eviction notice. On the other hand, you may lose the tenant anyway, and the sooner you begin eviction, the sooner a nonpaying tenant will get out and you'll be able to rerent to someone who will pay.

The Onetime Problem

In rare cases you may find that a tenant is late in paying the rent, but you're sure that the tenant will eventually pay and that *this is only a onetime problem.* If the tenants are responsible (i.e., they call you before you call them) and explain a onetime extenuating circumstance, you may want to allow them time to get the rent together. But be careful. If in the end they don't pay up, each day's delay is another day's rent lost, probably forever. Be absolutely sure you and your tenants agree on the final date when the rent is due and that there's a penalty included for the late payment. The penalty rams home the fact that late payment is not without consequences.

Extenuating Circumstances

I once had an excellent tenant who lived with her son, an airline pilot. She depended on her son's paycheck for the rent. One month he was in Saudi Arabia and his company sent his check to him there instead of to the house. She had to wait until he got back—nearly three weeks—before it could be straightened out. However, she didn't simply let things hang. She called me the day the rent was due and explained the situation. I agreed to wait and three weeks later, I got full payment.

The "Softy" Landlord

A word needs to be said about a landlord who feels sorry for his or her tenants' difficulties. A tenant may be out of work, sick, may have lost his or her wallet or whatever. You are a human being and you feel sorry for their troubles. You want to help them out and, unfortunately for you, the means to help them is so obvious and easy; you can just allow them to pay late. Just a few days late at first, then a week, then two, then maybe a month. . . It will help them out so much.

If you decide to operate your property as a charitable venture, that's fine. Just be sure that you know what you're doing up front and that you're prepared for the consequences (such as not being able to make your own mortgage, tax and insurance payments).

If you don't want to end up a pauper yourself, however, you'll very quickly realize that not only your profits but your financial survival require that you see yourself strictly as a businessperson.

If you simply can't overlook the plight of the helpless and the poor (who just happen to be occupying your house), I suggest you get out of the rental business at once. You don't belong as a landlord. You will lose money, become frustrated and probably earn yourself an early grave. Furthermore, you may even end up doing a disservice to those who come to you for help by inadvertently conspiring to lead them further into debt.

Tenants Are Tough

As a landlord, always remember that tenants are constantly sizing you up. If you look like a soft touch, you'll find that even the ones who pay regularly begin appealing to your sympathies. It may not be late rent; it could be repainting the premises in colors they prefer or adding new carpeting or even reducing the rent.

Furthermore, problem tenants, particularly those who have survived the threats and feeble actions of other less adroit landlords, can become quite skilled at taking advantage. They probe with late rent payments, unreasonable demands and even with threats to sue you if you don't comply with their wishes. They are looking for softness, and if they find it in you, you can be sure they will take full advantage of it.

Some tenants will put the rent payment last—after the car payment, clothing, bowling, eating out or whatever—if you let them. They may stop keeping up the property or may leave it a mess. Certainly not every tenant—not even most tenants—will do this. But there are enough who will, and it will change your hair from whatever color it now is to gray.

The Landlord's Rules

Here are some more rules that you should post next to the phone you use for making and receiving rental business calls.

Landlord's Rules #4–7 _____

Rule #4 The rent must always be paid first.

Rule #5 Always be soft-spoken and polite; never be seen as an aggressive person or as one who is out of control.

Rule #6 Whatever you give away in favors to the tenant, you probably will never get back.

Rule #7 There are no acceptable excuses for late rent.

One person to whom I showed these rules suggested that someone who followed them would be a compassionless person. I disagree.

Good tenants expect a landlord to act like one. I've been a tenant. I paid my rent on time. If I didn't, I fully expected the landlord to come around asking for it and would acknowledge that he or she had every right to demand it from me. If I couldn't pay or refused or simply spent the money elsewhere, I wouldn't blame the landlord a bit for giving me an eviction notice. I would deserve it! In fact, if the landlord overlooked my lateness or refusal to pay, I would have every right to think him or her a fool.

Next time you feel you're being too strict, reread the rules and the previous paragraph. Imagine how it was when you were a tenant (if you ever were). You'll find that suddenly you feel a lot stronger in your position as a landlord.

A Word about Receipts

When the tenant pays up, give them a receipt. They're entitled to one both morally and legally. Be sure, however, that the receipt specifies the time period for which the rent was paid. Putting in the exact time period—e.g., June 1 through June 30—avoids later confusion and argument over when the rent was paid.

If you receive part payment (e.g., two weeks), indicate the dates those weeks cover. Otherwise, if you later are forced to proceed with eviction, the tenant may claim that the partial payment was to cover the whole month, and your eviction proceedings may be delayed.

You're a Landlord—Be Proud of It

Once you become a landlord, for whatever reason, it becomes your job to collect rent, even when it's late. If you collect rent in a manner that is fair both to you and your tenants, you will find that not only do you prosper, but your tenants will respect you and in most cases pay promptly.

3

◆◆◆◆◆◆◆

When the Tenant Makes Unapproved Repairs or Improvements

One of the most shocking rental experiences I ever had was nearly 30 years ago when I stopped by a rental (actually one unit of a triplex) to collect the rent one day and was asked in by a friendly tenant who proudly displayed her new color scheme. I gasped in surprise and horror to see the walls and ceilings all painted a very shiny (and probably very permanent) deep purple.

The tenant saw my distress and immediately pointed out how well her black leather couch went with the new color scheme as did her very dark green throw rug. I had to agree that, indeed, the colors did seem in harmony.

What I was seeing, however, and the tenant wasn't, was my inability to rerent the unit when she moved out. Light colors normally make a place seem airy and roomy and are attractive to most people. There aren't many prospective tenants who are willing to move into a dark, cavelike dwelling. And painting over a dark color with a light color can be next to impossible, short of putting on three or four coats—an expensive proposition.

I dutifully informed the proud tenant that the rental agreement specifically forbade painting without the approval of the landlord and in any event, the landlord had to agree to the colors. The tenant just scoffed at that and said, "Who wouldn't like their place repainted, and by the way, what's wrong with the color?" What was I to do? After all, it was already painted!

I duly noted that when the tenant moved out, the unit would have to be repainted back to the original color and the cost would come out of the security/cleaning deposit, if there was enough. Then I left, hoping this tenant would stay there a very, very long time.

Avoiding Unapproved Repairs or Improvements

In the previous case the tenant disregarded a written part of the rental agreement and altered the property without the landlord's consent. Unfortunately, the landlord didn't find out until the deed was done, and by then it was too late to do anything except corrective work.

The lesson from this story is that you must nip this sort of thing in the bud. You want to head off unapproved work *before* it starts. Thus, you must emphasize your expectations from the very beginning, when the tenant first moves in.

Letting the Tenant Know What You Don't Want

Today when a tenant moves in, among other things discussed, I emphasize that there are to be no alterations, improvements or repairs to the property without the specific written approval of the landlord. I even highlight this part of the rental agreement and have the tenant initial it, indicating that they have indeed seen it. The wording may vary, but it often looks something like the following:

Repairs and Improvements

Tenants agree not to alter, redecorate or make repairs to the dwelling, except as provided by law, without first obtaining the owner's (landlord's) specific written permission.

Owner (landlord) agrees to undertake as soon as possible any and all repairs necessary to make the premises habitable and to correct any defects that are hazardous to the health and safety of the occupants, upon notification by tenants of the problem. If the owner (landlord) cannot reasonably complete such repairs within three days, he (she) shall keep tenants informed of the work progress.

The Tenant Who Asks to Paint

Assuming you've done your homework and have properly informed the tenant regarding your feelings about alterations, what do you do when the tenant calls up and says that he or she has been living in the property for three years now and the bedrooms, living room and dining room need to be repainted? The paint wasn't in wonderful condition (as you agree) when the tenant moved in, and it's time to repaint.

However, the tenant knows that repainting is costly, so they have a plan. If you will pay for the paint, they will do the work. Of course, you'll have control over the colors they choose.

The response to this seemingly fair request varies according to landlords and their experiences. Many landlords will acquiesce. I personally do not because I have found that most people are lousy painters. I include one of my sons and most of my relatives in this category.

In my experience, the average person doesn't do a good job of covering the whole wall or ceiling evenly with paint. They leave streaks, drips and bare spots on the trim. Often they accidentally get spray, drips and puddles on the floor and carpeting. In short, to have the average person paint my property usually means that not only will I have to have it repainted to get a good job, but I may also need to repair damage (such as paint on the carpet) along the way. Furthermore, once I agree to allowing the tenant to paint, any repainting and repairs are probably going to be out of my pocket.

At this point, I can hear other experienced landlords pooh-poohing what I've said. "Explain what you want. Show them how to paint. Tell the tenants that any damage to floors or carpets will come out of their deposit."

I've talked to many other landlords who have had perfectly good luck with this approach. I have, too, on occasion. But I've rented out enough units to see it go bad and when it does, it's a mess. Besides, once you give your permission to paint, you'll get a big argument from the tenant when you later try to charge them for cleanup.

If a property needs repainting, either I paint it myself or I hire a competent person (often a handyman). It usually doesn't take me long or cost me much, and I'm assured of the result.

If, however, you feel that you want to try saving money and decide to go forward and allow the tenant to paint, I have a good suggestion. Buy the paint, rollers and brushes yourself, and always buy the very best quality as it will go on more easily and cover better. It improves your odds of getting a good job.

Landlord's Rule #8

Don't let the tenant paint the property.

The Tenant Who Wants To Improve the Property

Many times a tenant will come to you with a request that sounds very reasonable. One of the most common requests I've run into in the Southwest has to do with lawn sprinklers (in other parts of the country the request is often to build a sun porch or deck).

The tenant is usually responsible for watering the lawn (unless you have a gardener). However, it's a time-consuming burden to run a hose out and turn on a portable sprinkler head. The tenant says that what's needed is underground sprinklers. If you will pay for the materials and perhaps a minimum hourly wage, they will do the work.

As a landlord, you should know that sprinklers are an absolute necessity as is an electric timer that turns them on automatically. It's the only way you have any assurance that your lawn will be watered regularly. In the Southwest you need sprinklers, and this may seem like a request from heaven.

My advice is not to give in to the temptation of having the tenants do the work. Although installing a sprinkler system only requires rudimentary plumbing skills, it does require some skill—and hard work. Besides, in most locales these days it also requires a building department permit. (You will, after all, be tapping into the potable water supply.)

Few tenants have the determination to dig the long holes (sometimes a foot deep) required for the pipes or really want to spend the several weekends the work will require. You may have tenants who get started, give it a good try and then end up leaving you with an unfinished and half-excavated yard. No, they won't complain (although they may think about moving), but it will be up to you to get someone (yourself or a professional) to complete the work. And finishing a botched job, quite frankly, is tougher than doing it correctly right from the start. Yes, it does cost money to do it right. But, do you really want it done wrong?

The same holds true for other projects that your tenants may come up with such as building a deck or patio cover, adding a greenhouse window, converting a bedroom to a family room (or vice versa) or anything else. My advice is to risk offending the tenants by just saying no.

Landlord's Rule #9

Never let the tenants make improvements or alterations to the property.

Tenants' Repair Rights

Those new to being a landlord may wonder at the language in the rental agreement noted earlier in this chapter that stresses that the owner (landlord) will make repairs promptly, even giving a deadline and notice that the tenant will be informed regarding the progress of work being done. Why let the tenant know you plan to promptly take care of work? After all, you may be short of funds when the work is required and may want to let it slip a week or so.

The reason for this is that many states have now enacted laws that allow a tenant to make repairs and then deduct the cost of those repairs from the next rent payment. These laws exist because in the past unscrupulous landlords have rented out premises where there was inadequate water, sanitary facilities or heating. The tenants paid the rent and then didn't receive the water, heat or working toilet they were entitled to. To get things working, in the past they might have had to make the repairs themselves out of their own pockets. To secure payment from the landlord, they would then have to go to court, where the outcome was always in doubt.

The tenant protection laws of many states, on the other hand, provide that if the landlord doesn't promptly make repairs that are necessary to bring the property up to a condition fit for human occupancy, the tenants can take self-help measures. They can make the repairs themselves and then deduct the cost from the next month's rent.

There usually are conditions tied to this self-help remedy. The tenant must have informed the landlord of the problem. The landlord must refuse to correct it in a reasonable amount of time. And the repairs usually must not cost more than one month's rent. The tenant often cannot use this self-help method more than once or twice a year. (Check with your state department of real estate to see the exact rules in your state.)

A Problem for the Landlord

At first glance, you might wonder what's the problem with having the tenant do the repair. After all, isn't the landlord getting the necessary work done, without having to take the trouble to do it himself or herself?

◆

What Happens When Tenants Hire Servicepeople?

I have a friend whom I'll call Hal (who will pop up occasionally in this book). Hal was the very worst landlord I ever knew. He ran into this very problem.

Hal had a number of properties, including a small house that he owned and rented out. One evening fairly late, the tenants called to say that the water heater had developed a leak. Water was running out the bottom of it and into the garage. They had called the gas company, which told them that the heater was no longer operative and they had shut it down. Now the tenants had no hot water.

Hal, who was home enjoying a ball game with a glass of Chablis, one of his favorite pleasures, told them, "Yeah, yeah, I'll get back to you on it." He continued to watch the game and promptly forgot about the tenants.

They called again the next morning, that afternoon and the following evening. Hal decided they were being pests, particularly since he felt they weren't paying enough rent anyhow. So he ignored them.

A few days passed. The tenants stopped calling, and Hal, involved in other pursuits, promptly forgot about the whole thing. . . . until the beginning of the next month when the tenants sent in the rent, or should have. The rent was $650 a month, and they sent him a check for $23 and a paid bill for $627 for having a new water heater installed. Needless to say, Hal went through the roof.

He raced over to the property and demanded to know what was going on. He had no intention of paying $627 for a water heater. He hadn't authorized it. Even if he did, he was sure he could get one installed for a few hundred dollars. Why, he could install it himself for half that!

The tenants, who had checked with a local real estate agent, calmly explained that they had called him seven times (Was it seven times, he wondered? Could it have been that many?) over a three-day period, and he had not responded. They couldn't live in the property without hot water. So, under the repairs by tenants laws of their state, they had fixed the problem. Since they felt it was an emergency (they didn't want to wait a week for a plumber's appointment), they called a serviceperson who came right out and did the work. They told Hal he would be pleased to know that the new water heater was one of the best produced and, of course, one of the most expensive.

This story illustrates the reason why you don't want to have your tenants make repairs. Their objectives are naturally going to be different from yours. They want the repairs done as quickly as possible, and cost is no object. You want them done in a timely manner, of course, but as inexpensively as possible.

Landlord's Rule #10

Never ignore tenants' requests for repairs involving habitability to the property. Always handle them promptly yourself.

4

•••◆•••

The Tenant Who Calls in the Middle of the Night

Some tenants can be pests. The trouble is, they can be good-paying pests.

Of course, it's always important to get to know your tenants so that if something goes awry, you'll know with whom you're dealing. It's a bit late to strike up a relationship when the tenant is fuming mad about something.

On the other hand, just as the tenants want to have the "quiet enjoyment" of your property, you as a landlord normally want to be isolated from their lives and small problems. Except in unusual circumstances (such as when you rent to relatives, an act of pure self-punishment), you should be friendly but not too friendly with your tenants. You want to be able to drop by or call up on the phone and hear a hearty "how are you doing?" on the other end. The idea is that you want your tenants to respect you, not love you; and more important, you don't want them to bring you into their lives.

◆————————————————————————————

Sally's Pesky Tenant

Another friend of mine, Sally, is a landlady who owns several houses. (She's also a real estate agent and should know better when it comes to dealing with tenants.) Not long ago Sally had a problem tenant. No, this tenant wasn't paying late or messing up the property. Rather, this tenant was calling Sally at all hours with problems that were trivial. For example, the tenant called Sally at 10:30 one evening to say a faucet was dripping. That's certainly something that needs to be fixed, but it's not an emergency that requires fixing at night. Sally sent a handyman over the next day and he took care of it.

Another evening at 11:30 the tenant called Sally to say that a doorstop had come off and the door handle was in danger of making a hole in the wall (a fairly common problem with rental property). Sally had the handyman go out a few days later. In the meantime the tenant called twice more about the same problem.

In fact, there was hardly a week that went by that the tenant didn't call once or twice with problems from a broken screen to a sprinkler head aimed in the wrong direction. Sally was ready to kick the tenant out because of the intrusions into her life. But the tenant always paid well, often in advance of the time the rent was due, and was always cordial when she called, treating Sally like an old friend asking for a small favor.

Eventually Sally solved the problem. At an additional cost, she had a management firm take over the property and she changed her phone number! (We'll have more to say about this alternative in Chapter 21.)

Getting Off on the Right Foot

The problem in the previous story stems from the fact that initially Sally struck up the wrong relationship with the tenant. The tenant was a single woman who was apparently lonely and looking for friends. Sally, being gregarious (a requirement for real estate agents), naturally commiserated with the woman about her problems, and by the time the woman moved in, she considered Sally a kindred spirit. Sally, on the other hand, simply thought she was being friendly in an agent's sort of way.

Soon after the tenant moved in, she began calling Sally, and at first Sally responded with her normal friendly demeanor, never realizing this was being misinterpreted by the tenant. Soon there was a one-way relationship established that was driving Sally crazy. The costly way out for Sally was to get someone else to take over management of the property.

Landlord's Rule #11

Always be friendly with your tenants; never be their friends.

A Business Proposition

From the first, you must establish that although you may be a friendly person, the landlord-tenant relationship is basically one of business. Yes, as a landlord you are available for handling problems that occur with the property—but at the normal business hours of 8:00 A.M. to 5:00 P.M. or in the early evening if you work during the day. If the tenant calls late in the evening, it has to be a real emergency that threatens the habitability of the property.

One landlord I know has cards printed up with his name, address and phone on them as well as his business hours. Since he works during the day, his business hours are from 6:00 to 9:00 in the evening. The phone line is just for rental calls, and he has an answering machine on the phone to take calls at other times. Since he frequently checks the answering machine during the day and can monitor calls after 9:00 P.M., he is able to keep up to date on any tenant requests or emergencies without having them intrude on his regular work or personal life.

The Demanding Tenant

Sometimes tenants aren't friendly—they're just demanding. These tenants may call at all hours of the day or night with problems that may or may not be legitimate complaints. For example, a tenant may call to complain about the color of paint in the living room—it doesn't go with their furniture and they want you to repaint. Or perhaps the garage doesn't have an automatic door opener and they want one installed. (Never mind that there was no door opener when they moved in, and they were aware of this fact.) Now they want one because lifting the door is just too hard, and they want you to immediately take care of it.

Or perhaps the sliding screen door leading to the patio doesn't slide easily enough on its track. It works fine and doesn't come off the track, but it doesn't function as smoothly as the tenant would like. Or a closet door creaks when it is opened. Or the dishwasher isn't getting the dishes clean enough.

The list can go on and on, but you get the idea. The demands are in a gray area. They certainly aren't threatening the habitability of the property. They don't qualify as true repairs. They aren't exactly alterations. They are sort of—but not quite—improvements.

Drawing a Line in the Sand

If you allow such a tenant to have his or her way, you will spend the entire period of the tenancy (and probably a great deal of money) making changes to the property that may not really be necessary from your perspective as a landlord. What you need to do is to make clear to the tenant what you are willing to do . . . and what you're not willing to take on. You need to draw a line in the sand and indicate that you won't step over it.

When I get the first such request from a tenant who is paying rent on time, I usually go along and have the change or the work done, assuming it isn't too costly. However, while the work is being done, I tell the tenant that this is not something I feel obligated to do, but I'm just doing it because they're such a good tenant. In the future, however, I won't do any more unnecessary work. I might say the following:

I'm greasing all of the door hinges [actually adding white graphite powder, as grease or oil drips and stains] so they won't squeak. I'm doing this only once because you're such good tenants. However, in any house the door hinges will always tend to squeak. In the future you'll have to take care of this yourself. I'll always fix anything that breaks, such as a broken furnace or a leaking faucet. But squeaky door hinges, a sliding screen door that works okay but doesn't move quite as smoothly as you want or a dishwasher that operates properly but doesn't get dishes quite as clean as you'd like are not broken items. Therefore, I won't fix them. If you want a new screen door or a new dishwasher, I can arrange to have them put in, but you'll have to pay for them yourself.

That usually ends the discussion. It also indicates what I'm willing to do and what I won't do. I've given the tenant my parameters. While some tenants might continue to "bump the envelope" to see what more they can wring out of me, most quickly understand the situation and stop being demanding. For those persistent complainers, doing one small job and sending them a bill for it, even if it's only ten dollars or so, quickly ends the demands.

Remember, if you lay down in the street, someone will walk on you. It's far better to be erect and let others know where you stand. Yes, once in a great while it might cost you a tenant, but the rest of the time you'll sleep peacefully at night without pesty phone calls.

5

•••◆•••

When the Tenant Doesn't Maintain the Property

There are two ingredients involved in getting the tenant to take good care of your property. The first is clarity—you have to make absolutely sure that your tenants are clear about what they are supposed to do. The second ingredient is to have reasonable expectations—you must make absolutely sure that your tenants can reasonably accomplish what you and they agree upon.

When a tenant doesn't keep the premises clean, mow the lawn, trim the trees, water the grounds, keep up the pool and in general maintain the property the way you feel it should be maintained, your first job is to determine whether it's an unreasonable expectation on your part or an impossible task for the tenant. Answering those two questions will often do far more than ranting and raving at the tenant for not doing the work.

◆————————————————

Hal's Unreasonable Expectations

Hal, whom we met in Chapter 3, wrote into his leases that his tenants were to pay for all utilities, including water. (Why should he pay for utilities that the tenant used?) In addition, on one enormous property in particular, he also emphasized that the tenants were to maintain the lawn and shrubs in the front and rear yards in good condition.

Hal rented the property during the early summer and a few months after the tenants moved in, he drove by, only to see that the lawn was brown and thinning and the leaves were falling off the shrubs. He stopped his car, jumped out and ran up to the door, startling the tenants by demanding to know why they were killing his lawn and shrubs.

They shrugged and said they had watered heavily the first month, until they got a water bill for $145. Since then, they were only watering minimally. If Hal wanted to pay the water bill, they'd water all he wanted. Otherwise, they couldn't afford to water.

Hal ranted and raved and threatened to throw them out for violating their lease. A month and a half later they moved on their own, leaving a dead lawn and dying shrubs that made rerenting much more difficult.

At the time you sign a rental agreement with a tenant, it's not enough that you both agree on who is to take care of what maintenance. It's also important that the agreement be reasonable and that the tenant be able to handle what you've both agreed upon.

Landlord's Rule #12

Never ask the tenants to take on more maintenance than they can handle.

In the case of watering lawns, Landlord's Rule #12 should be obvious. Many landlords will automatically pay for water just to be sure that lawns and shrubs are adequately maintained. Unfortunately, this sometimes leads to excessive use of water by the tenant. However, having a nice green front yard can be essential to rerenting the property, and you can't grow a lawn overnight. (Yes, you can plant sod and new shrubs, but that really isn't cost-effective.) Most landlords feel it's cheaper in the long run to pay the water bills than it is to run the risk of having the tenants let the greenery die out.

One exception to the rule is in drought areas where there's a hefty money penalty for using too much water. In such areas you might want to give your tenants a water allowance. You might pay $30 of the water bill (or whatever) a month for each month that you see that the yard is green.

Landlord's Rule #13

Never give rent deductions (discussed later in greater detail). For example, don't reduce the rent by $30 if the tenant waters the yard properly. Almost immediately the tenant will think of the rental rate as $30 less and will forget about what has to be done to earn that money. On the other hand, if you send a check *made payable to the water company* for $30 each month (e.g., so that the lawns are mowed and shrubs trimmed), you have a continuing incentive that is tied directly to the maintenance task you want accomplished. (Note: don't write the check to the tenant or you could fall under federal or state employer rules.)

The Messy Tenant

I've had tenants who kept the inside of the house or apartment so clean that the old expression "you could eat off the floor" was almost no exaggeration. And I've had tenants who made such a mess out of the premises that you had trouble walking between rooms, having to step over piles of debris. I, like you, prefer the former tenant; but if you rent long enough (and it won't take that long), you'll get the latter. What do you do about the messy tenant?

This is another good reason for stopping by your rental periodically and walking through. It doesn't have to be a formal appointment (although technically you do need to make an appointment to get in). Just drop by and ask how things are going. Mention that there was an old leak in one of the sinks and you want to check to be sure it's fixed, or you want to change the furnace filter. If you're on good relations with the tenant, you'll most certainly be asked in. Now you can look around.

Mess versus Damage

Some people are just not very neat, and there's nothing you can do about it. For example, they may allow clothes to fall everywhere. I once had a tenant who had a "clothes room." That meant that all her clothes were dumped on the floor of one room—some clean, some dirty, some needing ironing. You get the idea. At times the clothes piles in that room seemed three feet deep or more!

Landlord's Rule #14

Don't insist that your tenants follow your lifestyle or your family rules. You will only become ineffectual and frustrated.

That's not the way our family is run, and I don't think any family should be run that way. But it's also none of my business how other families are run, and I know that. As long as there was no damage to the property (and there wasn't), I couldn't say anything, except weakly point out a possible fire hazard.

◆

Unfixed Damage Can Be Expensive and Dangerous

Sally, whom we met in Chapter 4, was called by her tenants one day to say that their son had driven a baseball through one of two large plateglass windows in the back of the residence. They wanted it fixed immediately, as jagged pieces of glass were all over.

Sally immediately sent over a glazer who took care of the window, for $350. Then she paid for the repair out of the tenant's security deposit and sent a bill for that amount, requesting the tenants bring their security deposit back up to its full level. They were outraged at the price (it was safety glass) but agreed to pay.

The real story started a month later when Sally dropped by for a surprise visit. The tenants invited her in, and she immediately noticed that the *other* plateglass window was also broken. (Their son apparently was a strong, but not highly accurate, baseball player.) However, they had not reported it. Instead, they had taken several sheets of transparent tape and had taped up the broken shards to hold the broken window together. They casually mentioned that it was a lot cheaper than replacing it.

Sally said it was a tremendous safety hazard and told them it had to be fixed. She also immediately sent them a note repeating what she had said. She gave them one week to correct the problem on their own, or she would hire someone to come in and fix the window and would charge it to them.

The tenants took care of the window, but they no longer invited her inside when she casually dropped by. So now Sally makes an appointment to stop by once every other month or so. (Your rental agreement should contain a clause allowing you to enter and examine the property upon giving the tenant adequate notice—usually 24 hours.) In any event, there are no more broken windows.

Damage is quite different from a mess. When a property has been damaged, you must make it perfectly clear to the tenant that they must immediately correct the problem or you will correct it and charge them for it. Damage requiring immediate correction includes any of the following:

- Broken glass

- Paint or heavy crayon marks on walls, often caused by allowing children to run free with crayons or paints. (Crayons in particular can be hard to remove since they often stain right through wall paint. If you don't catch this immediately, it may occur on many more walls during the tenancy.)

- Animal urine or feces anywhere inside the property, except in a special animal litter box

- Broken sinks, stoves, faucets, heaters, floor tiles

- Large holes in walls, torn drapes or window coverings (that you have provided)

Note: normal wear and tear, including small paint or crayon marks, small holes to walls (particularly behind door knobs), dirty drapes or window coverings, dirty sinks, stoves, etc., is the only kind of damage that doesn't require immediate correction.

Maintenance Tasks You Should Let the Tenant Do

There are several maintenance tasks that tenants usually expect to do and that landlords assign to them.

Yard Maintenance

When you are renting out a single-family dwelling, a duplex (two units) or a triplex (three units), it is quite common to have the tenants take care of the yard, both front and back. If a tenant balks, a good way of handling the situation is to offer to hire a gardener but to add the cost to the monthly rent. (Some landlords ask for a higher rent and then offer to negotiate a lower rent if the tenant will agree to take care of the yard work. In either case, it is important that the tenant understand his or her responsibilities.)

When you are renting smaller multiple units (small apartment buildings or in some cases, duplexes, triplexes or even fourplexes where there are common areas), you may want to give one tenant a lower rent for sweeping, cleaning and, if the total areas are small, mowing and gardening. This avoids problems of who is supposed to take care of what area. For bigger buildings, it is almost always advisable to hire a gardener.

Minimal Plumbing Work

This also is sometimes taken care of by tenants who express a willingness and who have plumbing ability. This includes unstopping plugged toilets or drains, changing washers in faucets, cleaning heating filters and so on. I have one tenant who is more than happy to do all of these things just so I won't bother to come around. This tenant loves his privacy.

Cleaning of Kitchens, Baths and Floors

The tenant should maintain the property in at least a clean enough condition so that there are no health hazards. Also, tenants who keep a place filthy aren't likely to leave it very clean when they move out, and it may cost more than their cleaning deposit to put it back into shape.

Maintenance Tasks You Should Never Let the Tenant Do

This list of tasks is far longer. It includes the following:

- *Cleaning out plugged drain lines.* A plugged drain line can be a more serious problem than a plugged sink or toilet. A long mechanical rooter device is required, and it's most easily handled by professionals.

- *Painting.* This was already discussed in Chapter 4.

- *Washing walls.* Walls get dirty over time. Washing them only makes the dirt stand out more. The reason is that you can't really wash a wall very effectively. You can only wash a portion of it, usually the lower half and then only sections. That means that where the washed and unwashed areas meet, there will be visible dirt lines. I always discourage tenants from washing walls. When they are dirty, they need to be both cleaned and repainted.

- *Fixing anything major that goes wrong, such as a water heater, furnace, air conditioner, compactor or garbage disposal.* Your liability if the tenant gets hurt doing work you authorize could be enormous. Also, while the tenant may have good intentions, he or she may not be competent to do a good job.

- *Taking care of pools and spas.*

Pool Maintenance Is for Professionals

Our poor friend Hal had a most unfortunate experience. He owned a property with a large pool and was paying $75 a month to a pool service company to maintain it. One day his tenant suggested that Hal turn over the pool maintenance to the tenant. "It only costs $5 or $10 worth of chemicals each month, and I'm here anyway. Just cut the rent by $40 a month. We'll both save money that way."

Hal jumped at the opportunity, but when he came back to the property several months later, he was aghast at the pool's condition. It had been bright blue. Now it was green with yellow and black algae growing profusely on the sides. He demanded to know what had happened.

The tenant sheepishly confessed that he tried to save money on chlorine and probably hadn't added enough. He told Hal, however, that he'd cure it.

Hal came back a month later, and it was even worse. The tenant admitted he couldn't handle the pool and said Hal had better take back its maintenance.

The real problem is that when Hal called his pool service company back, they told him they would have to drain the pool, acid-wash it several times and even replace some of the filtration equipment. It would cost him big bucks—close to a thousand dollars.

The point to make about Hal's story is that taking care of a pool or spa is not the simple task that most people think it is. It requires constant attention and the right kind of care. If you let it go, you can ruin the pool. I know of one person who let a pool in a rental go without maintenance for six months. When he finally tried to have it cleaned up, he was told that the algae had eaten into the plaster walls. The plaster had to be sandblasted off, and then new plaster was put on. It cost him over $6,000 to get the pool reconditioned!

Yes, some tenants may be capable of maintaining your pool. But are you willing to risk the potential damage if they don't do their job or do it poorly? Besides, we haven't even gone into the health hazards that exist. What if a tenant or his or her child is burned by the harsh chemicals used (i.e., chlorine and acid)?

◆ **CAUTION**   If you reduce rent, forego the acceptance of rent or pay a tenant directly for performing work such as maintaining a pool, you could actually be setting up an employee-employer relationship as defined by federal and perhaps even state law. If such a relationship exists, you could be responsible for withholding tax, workmen's compensation and other employer responsibilities. Check with your attorney.

The next time a tenant proposes to take over pool or spa maintenance, think twice about it. Maybe even think three times.

PART TWO

Getting and Keeping Better Tenants

6

$$\bullet\bullet\bullet\blacklozenge\bullet\bullet\bullet$$

Advertising That Gets Results

You've got a rental; you want a tenant. What could be more necessary? Yet, how do you get from point A to point B? How do you find just the right tenant?

The answer, of course, is that you advertise. The trouble is that most people think advertising only means putting an ad in the local newspaper. Although this is a primary method of getting the word out about your rental, there may be other, less expensive methods as well.

The Sign

Don't ever overlook or downplay the importance of a sign on your property. Over the years I've probably gotten as many as a third of all my tenants simply from a sign placed in front of the property (or put in a window, in the case of a condo).

The reason a sign works so well is that there often are prospective tenants who want to live in your area who cruise the area looking for rentals. In many cases, in fact, as soon as you put out a sign—perhaps even the first day—you'll have people stopping by to ask about the property.

The sign itself doesn't have to be fancy. It just has to get the message across. A typical rental sign may be as simple as this:

```
┌─────────────────────┐
│                     │
│                     │
│     FOR RENT        │
│     555-3465        │
│                     │
│                     │
└─────────────────────┘
```

You may, of course, add additional information, such as the number of bedrooms and the price. I advise against advertising your price *on the sign*. The reason is that the people looking at the sign only see the outside of the house. (Unless you're there to show the rental, it's locked up.) You may eliminate potential tenants who think the rental is either too high or too low based on the way the outside looks. But they can't know the real value until they see the inside, and they won't accomplish that until they call you. Thus, advertising the price on *the sign* can work against you.

Besides, I think putting out the price cheapens the property. It's almost like saying that the price is the *only* reason to rent the property, not it's design, size, cleanliness or other outstanding features.

◆ **CAUTION**   Make it perfectly clear that if you're in the process of painting or fixing up the property, the way it currently looks is not the way it will look when you're ready to rent. Therefore, it's a good idea to put a date on the sign—for example, "Available 6/30." This also alerts tenants who have to move from their current house as to when they can move into yours. (See more on this in Chapter 12.)

The Neighborhood Flyer

The problem with just using a sign is that unless someone happens to drive down your street, they won't see it. Unless your street is heavily trafficked, your sign alone won't do the job.

◆

A Missed Opportunity

This came home to me many years ago when I was trying to rent a house using a sign and a newspaper ad. After almost a month, I finally rented the property to a marginal tenant. (By then I was desperate.)

No sooner had the new tenant started moving in than a neighbor from the house behind mine (and on a different street) stopped by to say she saw the moving van and how sorry she was that she hadn't known my house was for rent. Her cousin and his wife were new to the area and were looking for just the sort of house I had. He had a great job, they had great credit and . . . you get the picture.

Since then I have made sure that all the neighbors know when I have a property for rent.

Whenever I have a rental, I create a very brief flyer, as shown in Figure 6.1, describing the property and run off a hundred or more at the local copy store. Then I hire a neighborhood kid to leave a flyer at the doors of all the houses nearby. (Be careful to instruct your delivery person not to put them in mailboxes. The U.S. Post Office won't tolerate anything in a mailbox that isn't properly stamped.) Thus, all the neighbors will know that the house is for rent and can send any prospective tenants by.

The flyer can be handwritten or typed, and copying only costs about five dollars per 100 copies. The flyers usually cost no more than ten dollars to distribute.

Too Soon/Too Late

Timing is critical in finding tenants. Rents are usually up at the end of the month. That means that tenants wanting to move from their current rental will be looking to move on or around the first of the month. Thus, they'll be shopping for a new rental a few weeks before. (This is also critical when placing your newspaper ad, as we'll see later in this chapter.)

FIGURE 6.1   Typical Rental Flyer

FOR RENT!

(You can paste in a picture of the
house for greater impact.)

1234 Titus Street
3 Bedrooms, 2 Baths
$750*

Den, Fireplace, Repainted, New Carpets
Call 555-5465
Available 10/1

Note: Putting the price on the flyer, unlike the sign, is a good idea. It doesn't cheapen the property and it helps them know if it's in their range.

Thus, it's a good idea to get your flyers (and your sign) out there early. You can get the flyer out by the 15th and indicate that the property won't be available until the 1st.

Landlord's Rule #15 _____

Always try to rent your properties from the 1st to the 1st.
(Most tenants are available to move in on the 1st. If you try to

rent from the 15th, they will want the rent to start on the 1st anyway and you could lose two weeks payment.)

Bulletin Boards

People read bulletin boards at supermarkets, pharmacies and other neighborhood centers. You may want to tack one of your flyers up on a bulletin board. (Some boards only allow three-by-five-inch index cards, so you may have to cramp the information on to one of those cards.)

A better source is bulletin boards at the housing or personnel offices of local companies. Often there are two or three major employers in the nearby area. Call and ask if you can hang a flyer on their boards. Most will be happy to oblige. (Sometimes it's a good idea to hang four or five flyers with a pushpin. That way, someone interested can take one and leave the rest for other prospective tenants.)

One problem with bulletin boards, particularly in public areas such as shopping malls, is that you're also announcing that your house is vacant to an element who may only be interested in breaking in, having a party at your house or stealing appliances, drapes or whatever. This is probably a remote possibility in most areas, but in some high-crime areas you may just want to forget the bulletin board idea.

High-Tech Bulletin Boards

There's another kind of bulletin board that's high tech and that most landlords don't even think about. It's extremely effective because of its novelty. I'm speaking of computer bulletin boards.

Many boards that can be reached by a computer/modem offer a separate area for real estate sales or rentals. Often these areas are seldom if ever used. However, they may be scrutinized by people who have an interest in them—namely, buyers and tenants.

If you take advantage of these electronic boards, you may find a virtually free source of advertising. Besides, you'll at least know that the prospective tenant who found you this way is computer-literate!

Yet another high-tech bulletin board is found on local cable access channels. These channels will often allow you to list a property for rent for a nominal fee. They may only give you five seconds to flash a notice.

But people watch these channels, and the novelty of seeing a rental advertised can attract widespread attention and find you a choice tenant.

List with Agents

Landlords sometimes forget that real estate agents not only sell but also rent property. Real estate agents, particularly those in big offices, often have a steady stream of calls from tenants looking for rentals.

Agents like rentals because they sometimes can convert prospective tenants to buyers as well as landlords to sellers. Often an agent will take on your property and handle the rental for just the cost of advertising.

Some agents, however, will want to list your property on the Multiple Listing Service (MLS) or other cobrokering exchange. This means that they will split a commission with another broker who may find a tenant.

Listing with agents gives your property much more exposure. However, it is probably the most expensive method of getting a tenant. The reason is that the typical fee is a full month's rent. That's right, you pay the agent (or agents) one month's rent to find you a tenant.

Of course, the agent also may qualify the tenant and guarantee that the tenant will stay put for a period of time. If the tenant moves out within six months, for example, the agent may refund a part of the fee or find a new tenant for free or, at least, a reduced fee.

In a tight market where there are few tenants and lots of rentals, you may want to consider this alternative. After all, you don't pay unless the agent finds you a tenant.

Fee Lists

Some agents also put out a list of rentals area by area. They charge prospective tenants a fee for this list, which is usually updated weekly. Since getting on a list is often free to landlords, there's no harm in having your property listed there.

Newspaper Advertisements

By far the most widely used advertising medium for rental properties is classified ads in newspapers. On some Sundays at the end of the month the rental ads may cover many pages. But that, of course, is the problem. Your ad is in direct competition with everyone else's ad in the newspaper. The other problem is the cost. Advertising your property in the newspaper can be very costly—perhaps the most expensive form of advertising you can use.

Tenants, however, often look to the newspaper as their first source of information about rentals. Therefore, you will be hard-pressed not to advertise (unless your sign or flyer worked very well for you). Your goal, however, becomes effectiveness and, of course, keeping the cost down.

Effective Newspaper Ads

To get the biggest bang for your buck, think like a tenant. What sort of advertising would a tenant read?

What Paper?

Don't advertise in the big city paper. It costs too much and covers too big an area. Just like buyers looking to purchase a house, tenants look for area first. They often look specifically within a single residential development or even a much smaller area. Many big city papers cover the downtown area and all suburbs. If you're paying for advertising that's reaching people completely out of your area, you're wasting your money.

On the other hand, you can also find smaller local papers, weeklies, journals, shoppers' guides (given away free), penny-savers and so on. These are typically aimed at a very small shopping area. If you were looking for a rental in a specific area, wouldn't you look in these sources first?

To find them, check at local grocery stores, which often carry them. Also ask the neighbors or your current tenant who is moving out. They usually can tell you which are the more popular papers.

Don't be afraid to advertise in a small paper or one that's filled with ads and not many articles. These are often the very best sources of tenants for you.

How Big?

Don't believe the old maxim, "bigger is better." When it comes to rental advertising, "bigger" just means costlier, not better.

Think of it from the tenants' perspective. They are looking for the best, least expensive rental they can find. Someone who takes out a large display ad is in effect saying, "I can afford to place big, costly ads. Therefore, it stands to reason that I have to charge more for my rental!"

Prospective tenants look for the smallest ads. Therefore, that's what you need to get. I rarely put in an ad that has more than three or four lines. That's more than enough to get my message across.

Landlord's Rule #16 _____

Less is more when it comes to classified advertising.

How Often?

Run your ad as often as possible. However, pick and choose when to run it, and change it frequently.

No, that's not as contradictory as it sounds. The idea is to run your ad when tenants are looking. As noted earlier, most tenants move around the end of the month. Therefore, most are already moved in by the first or second week of the month and relatively few are looking. Thus, your ads will generally reach fewer prospective tenants during the first or second weeks of the month. Conserve your money. Either don't advertise early in the month or run a smaller ad. (If you have your act together, you'll rent from the 1st to the 1st and advertise from the middle of the month *before* your property becomes vacant.)

The best time to catch tenants looking at ads is the middle to end of the month—the last two weeks of the month. (You will notice that rental ads typically will be heavier then.) But don't run the same ad for more than two weeks. If you don't catch a tenant after two weeks, change the ad. Otherwise, those who are looking will remember your ad and say to themselves, "That place must be a dog. They can't get it rented!"

What do you do if you haven't caught a tenant during the last two weeks of the month? If you want to continue running newspaper ads, run the minimum ad—i.e., usually two lines. It's just enough to give you exposure. Also concentrate on the other methods mentioned previously.

What To Say

The hardest part of placing a classified ad for most people is figuring out what to say. The problem usually is one of perspective—the landlord's versus the tenant's. Most landlords tend to write down things they like about the rental instead of realizing that what should go into the ad are only things that tenants find attractive. For example, the landlord may like a small yard because of reduced maintenance problems, but tenants may be looking for a big yard for their kids to play in. Or the landlord may be thinking of the new double-pane insulated glass windows he recently installed to save on heating and cooling costs, while the tenant wants to know that there are clean drapes and carpeting.

Think Benefits

When you're working to put together the words for your ad, think only about the benefits your rental offers a tenant. If you write down renter benefits, you really can't go wrong.

Landlord's Rule #17

Always emphasize tenant benefits when you're trying to rent up your property.

What are tenant benefits? Here are some of the things tenants look for:

- *Location.* Mention a desirable neighborhood or school and whether it is close to shopping, buses and freeways.

- *Size.* Give the number of bedrooms. Mention if the house or lot is oversized or if there are extra rooms, such as a family room.

- *Amenities.* Mention a fireplace, spa, pool, appliances or other desired items that go with rental.

- *Cleanliness.* Say if the rental is newly painted, has new carpeting or drapes or is especially clean.

From this list one might think that an ad would have to be a dozen lines long to include all of a rental's features. That's not really the case, partly because just a mention will do and also because there are abbreviations that are commonly understood. For example, here's an ad that has benefits from each category:

> **Acacia Schools—3 bdrm.**
> **2 bath, oversize fam. rm.,**
> **spa, frplc., just repainted.**
> **$675. 555-4321**

Abbreviate

The following is a list of commonly understood abbreviations you can use to shorten your ad (and thus reduce its cost):

Bedroom—bdrm

Fireplace—frplc

dishwasher—dshwshr

townhouse—twnhs

washer/dryer—wshr/dryr

Garage—gar

large—lg

small—sml

Don't be afraid to use abbreviations, but note that some newspapers may restrict the abbreviations they allow. Just be careful that the abbreviations you do use are understandable. For example, I was recently reading the rental ads in the local paper and came across this strange ad:

> **Fr. Rt.—3b/2b, chc lcl, $500.**
> **555-8979**

Does "Fr. Rt." mean "Free Rent" or "For Rent"? Is it three bedrooms or two? What is "chc lcl"? Chocolate? (Actually, I think the ad meant to say, "For Rent—3 bedrooms, 2 baths, choice location. . . .")

If there's some question about what you mean, always use the long form.

The Hook

Every ad needs a hook. This is the word or words at the beginning that catch the reader's attention and force him or her to read the rest of what you have to say.

Generally speaking, your hook should be the best benefit your rental offers. In the previous ad, it was the location. However, it could be almost anything. The following list includes some great words you can use to hook potential tenants who are reading ads:

Oversize house

Close to schools (or "close in")

5-bedrooms (emphasizing size)

Room to roam (oversize lot)

Just remodeled

Freshly painted

New carpets and drapes

Garden living

Quiet cul-de-sac

You get the idea. Pick out the biggest benefit to your reader and stress it.

Don't Be Afraid of the Short Ad

It's possible to get away with a two-line ad. (Remember, the ad is already appearing in a rental section of the paper, often under a specific area and type of property, such as condo.) For example:

New Paint—3bdrm/2bath,
$675, 555-4993

The trouble is that if it's a competitive market, you won't be likely to draw many responses. Other landlords with bigger, more descriptive ads will command the most attention. On the other hand, when the rental market is good (for landlords), almost any ad will do, even one this tiny.

Don't Sell the Obvious

Sometimes you have to go for the second-best benefit because the first is obvious. For example, your paper may list rentals by neighborhood or local area. Your biggest benefit may be that your property is in the choice Westwood area. But you're already advertising in the section under "Westwood." You don't need to say it again. List the next biggest benefit. Maybe you have one of the biggest homes in the area or it has just been repainted. Go with that.

The Price

Always mention the price when you don't give the address. (Don't give the address in an ad unless you or a manager are always there to receive prospective tenants.) You not only want to get as many potentially acceptable tenants as possible to call, but you also want to eliminate as many who can't afford or won't want your property. Price is the great leveler.

Discounted Newspaper Ads

Don't overlook the possibility of getting discounted advertising. The most expensive ad you can place is the one for a single day. Newspapers usually will give discounts for longer placement. Sometimes it only costs a few dollars more to run an ad for a week than for a day. Similarly, two weeks can be only a few dollars more on top of that. (I wouldn't run the same ad for more than two weeks as it will get stale and stop attracting calls.) You'll probably have to run the ad for a week or two anyway, so why not sign up for it at the beginning and save money?

The same holds true for lines. A single line is typically the most expensive ad. In many instances three lines can be purchased for just a few dollars more than one line.

Also consider special sections. Sometimes newspapers will have deep classified advertising discounts for rentals that are below a certain price—for example, below $300 or below $500.

Beware of Offering Move-In Discounts

Sometimes the rental market really gets bad. There are just too many properties chasing too few tenants. When that happens, landlords, particularly those who have many rentals such as apartment building owners, will cut their prices and then begin offering move-in discounts. For example, ads may start appearing that say, "First Month's Rent Free!" or "Free TV To Move In!"

In these markets there evolves a kind of professional tenant who chases after the discounts. These tenants stay a month or two, long enough to get the promotion, and then move on to the next desperate landlord. You don't want this kind of tenant. You want a tenant who is willing to rent for a long period of time (hopefully for at least a year). If you are in a really tight market, it's better to lower the rent and get a good solid tenant than to try to "buy" a tenant with discounts.

Summary

In the final analysis your advertising, whether it's a sign or a classified ad, is your entrée into the world of tenants. It's your first step toward getting just the right kind of tenant. If you're aggressive about advertising, you'll rent your property faster and get a higher-quality tenant who will stay longer.

Landlord's Rule #18 _____

No tenant is better than having a bad tenant.

_____

7

◆◆◆◆◆◆

Responding to Tenants Who Call on Your Ad

There's an entire art (if not a science) involved with talking to prospective tenants over the phone. If you master this art, you'll find you have no trouble getting just the tenant you want. On the other hand, if you don't, you'll find yourself spinning your wheels, wasting time with unqualified tenants and worse, renting to tenants who end up not paying the rent. Get your phone response act together, and you'll save all kinds of problems down the road.

There are really only three steps to handling the phone when prospective tenants call. These steps are simple and easy to master, and they will go a long way toward ensuring that you get just the tenant you're looking for.

◆ **CAUTION** Be sure you're aware of the antidiscrimination laws (noted in Chapter 9) before taking any calls.

Step 1: Encourage the Hesitant Caller

When a prospective tenant calls on the phone, they may be just a little bit nervous and/or guarded. They usually want to find out as much information from you about your rental as they can before giving you any information about them. The reason is that they are screening out the bad rentals. They don't want to waste time, and they don't want some poor landlord with an unimpressive rental to try to talk them into renting something they don't want.

This hesitant approach doesn't mean you're talking to a potentially bad tenant. Quite the opposite, it probably means you're talking to someone who is sincerely interested in finding just the right property to rent. As with fishing, you're getting a nibble. Now the art is to turn that nibble into a real bite.

I suggest you encourage the hesitant caller. The way you do this is to be polite and answer the tenant's questions as fully and carefully as possible. Your goal is to give the tenant enough information to get hooked. Then you must reel him or her in with questions of your own.

Step 2: Sell the Property

You need to promote your property—to sell it to the tenant. After all, it's the only product you have. The tenant will almost always ask the following basic questions:

- How many and how big are the bedrooms?

- Does it have a large kitchen, family room or yard?

- Is it clean?

- Does it have a big garage?

- Do you take pets?

They may, of course, also ask some rather specific questions geared to their specific needs. If your property has a pool, they may ask if it has a separate fence and gate surrounding it—a real concern for tenants who have small children. They may ask if you have 220-volt electrical outlets in the laundry room because they have an electric dryer. They may ask if your house is near a particular bus route they need to use.

The art here is to amplify your answer and then turn it around into an innocuous question. After all, you're just as interested in qualifying the tenant as the tenant is in qualifying the property. For example, when answering how many bedrooms your property has or their size, you might say something such as, "It has three bedrooms, all good sized. The master is 14 feet by 12 feet. Is that big enough for your needs? How many people will be occupying the property?" Or you might respond, "The house is located near the L-123 bus line, and there's also I-405 freeway access nearby. Is that close enough? Do you work nearby?" Or you might say, "It has a large three-car garage with separate doors and openers for each car. Were you planning to work on cars in the garage, or do you have a lot of extra stuff to store?"

You get the idea. After you've established rapport by answering a few questions directly, you can begin to turn each answer into a question of your own. Soon enough you'll be learning as much about the tenant as he or she will about your property.

If the tenant seems happy with your description of the property and you seem happy with the would-be tenant's responses, work the conversation around to meeting the tenant at the premises. That way the tenant can see if he or she likes it, and you can qualify the tenant further.

Landlord's Rule #19

When a prospective tenant calls, the aim of your conversation should always be to get the tenant to the property. You can't sign a rental agreement over the phone.

Beware of the Professional Tenant's Call

Sometimes you'll get a call from someone who seems to know more about your property than you do. This tenant knows the area, the house and insists that you are charging too much but will consider renting from you for a lesser amount. In other words, he or she wants a concession over the phone.

Beware of such tenants. They are nothing but trouble. You may indeed want to give rent or other concessions to get a particularly good tenant, but you can't do that after one phone conversation and before qualifying a tenant in writing. Tenants who want small concessions early on often want bigger ones later. They may be the very tenants who hopscotch from landlord to landlord—just the sort you don't want.

Step 3: Qualify the Tenant

Finally, there's the matter of deciding whether you're even interested in showing the property to a prospective tenant. You need to have certain qualifying questions in mind ahead of time.

In Chapter 9 we'll discuss antidiscrimination considerations and some of the ways you can't discriminate against tenants. But for now, let's just say that you can determine the maximum occupancy of your property (though you can't refuse to rent to tenants just because they have children), you can decide if your tenants will be smokers or nonsmokers, you can refuse to rent to people who have pets or certain types of pets (but not Seeing Eye dogs) and you can require tenants to have minimum cash and financial qualifications. You can get at least an idea of how your tenant fits into all of these categories over the phone.

If the caller doesn't have enough money to move in, doesn't want to move in when your unit is ready, has too many family members for the size of the unit or otherwise is disqualified, you are wasting your time if you show them the property. You wouldn't want them as a tenant anyhow.

Minimum Tenant Qualifications

The following list presents some minimum qualifications that you may want to consider when a prospective tenant calls on your property:

- Tenant is willing to move in when your rental is ready.
- Tenant has the appropriate number of people in his or her family.
- Tenant has the cash available to pay all rent and deposits.
- Tenant has no pets or only those pets you allow.

Landlord's Dilemma

You must ask the prospective tenant about their financial condition and if they have the cash to move in. However, you don't want to chase away someone who's just calling over the phone by appearing to be too nosy. One answer is to say right up front what's needed to move in. For example, after you've talked for awhile and otherwise prequalified the prospective tenant, you might say, "The total move-in is the first month's rent of $750 plus a $750 cleaning deposit or $1,500. Is that going to be okay for you?" If the would-be tenant says it's no problem, you can proceed to show the property. On the other hand, if there's hemming and hawing and asking if part can be paid now and the rest in three weeks, you've probably eliminated this tenant.

Get the Tenant to the Property

As noted earlier, it's all for naught until the tenant actually sees the property and you see the rental application. Thus, getting the tenant to your property is the next step.

I may say something such as this to get the conversation going where I want it to go, "You sound as though you'd like the property I have for rent. Why don't I meet you there in 15 minutes and show it to you? You can then look it over and see if it's really something that will meet your needs."

Ask If There's a Problem

If the tenant seems hesitant to run out to the property, particularly after you've chatted for awhile and they seem to like what you've said (and you like what they've said), you should ask if there's a problem. You can be perfectly blunt. If there is a problem, it's best to get it out on the table before you spend any more time on this tenant. You can say something such as, "Is there some problem here that we haven't touched upon? You seem hesitant."

At this point the prospective tenant with a problem might blurt out any number of amazing things, such as, "Well, I didn't want to mention it, but I have a horse." Or, "You see, I'm having a fight with my present landlord about the three months I'm behind on my rent." Or, "I actually have seven kids, but I'm sure we'll all fit in your one-bedroom unit." Or, "I plan to run an auto body repair shop out of the garage. Is that okay?"

If you don't ask, you won't know.

Get the Tenant's Name and Phone Number

If you're going to run out to show the property, the least you want to know is that there's a reasonably good chance the prospective tenant will show. If they're willing to give their name and number over the phone, it's a pretty good indication they'll meet you. Besides, if they don't show, you want to be able to call and ask what happened. Or, you could be delayed and may need to call and arrange a different time.

Sometimes landlords are afraid to ask for a name and phone number from someone who just calls about an ad for fear of scaring them away. My feeling is that if a prospective tenant won't give you these basics, there's not really all that much chance they'll even show up to see the property.

Give Out the Address

Sometimes a prospective tenant will say they are interested but want to drive by the property to see if they like the location and neighborhood. They'll ask for the address.

I have no problem with this. In fact, I find it saves me a lot of time. If the would-be tenant has already driven by, has seen where the rental is located and finds it acceptable, I'm way ahead when I go out there to show the property. I'm almost guaranteed the person will show up.

In fact, if after talking to a would-be tenant on the phone and satisfying myself that this person is a likely candidate, I will often suggest they drive by and then, if interested, call me back. These callbacks are very frequently people who really want to rent.

The danger, of course, is that by giving out the address you expose your property to people who might want to trash an empty house or break in to steal things. But, they did call first and give you their phone number. (You can call back to confirm.) Yes, there's some risk. But, then again, there always is.

8

•••◆•••

Eye-Catching Property Preparation

A prospective tenant calls on your ad and after talking for a few minutes, you think this might be a good one. You arrange to meet with the person at the property in half an hour. You've done your job; now it's up to the property to sell itself. But will it?

Some landlords make the serious mistake of thinking that they're doing a tenant a favor by providing a rental. They figure it's up to the tenant to get the property into habitable shape. On the other hand, other landlords feel that a new tenant is like a guest coming into their house. They scrub and clean as if they were expecting their son's new bride to be spending the night.

Getting a property to the point where it will appeal to a prospective tenant is somewhere in between. In this chapter we'll consider what you can do, what you should do and what you can forget about doing.

◆ The Unfinished Cleaning Job

Our friend Hal had a house he was trying to rent. The last tenant had left it a bit of a mess, and Hal realized he couldn't rent it as it was. So he hired a service to come in and clean the entrance hall, living room and kitchen—those areas that prospective tenants first saw. The service did a reasonably good job and when the prospective tenants came in, they were suitably satisfied with the premises . . . until they went to the bathrooms, particularly the one off the master bedroom. There were bottles and creams spilled around, the sink had hairs in it and the toilet hadn't been cleaned. You get the idea. Needless to say, Hal was fuming at those "finicky people who expect me to do everything for them." The house stayed unrented until Hal finally called the service back to finish the job.

The moral of the story is that you have to do a good, thorough job of cleaning if you want to get a good tenant.

Must Do

Perhaps the best way to primp up your property so that it will appeal to a prospective tenant is to separate those areas that you must work on from those you can forget. Let's consider the "must do" areas first.

Entry

Clean or repaint the front door. Be sure the door handle is clean and that the entryway is swept. If possible, put a new floor mat down.

First impressions are critical. The first thing the prospective tenant sees is the entry. Be sure it looks great. A new coat of paint on the front door only takes a few moments, and it can make a world of difference.

Living Room, Dining Room, Hallways, Bedrooms

Shampoo the carpet and polish the floors. Paint any walls that have marks on them. Clean the windows and window coverings.

In most rentals carpets cover most of the floor space. A newly shampooed carpet makes the entire room look fresh. On the other hand, a "lived on" carpet looks dirty and worn, even if it's fairly new. Good tenants like things clean, and a clean carpet is very important.

Walls that have marks on them look old, worn and dirty and are a real distraction. Paint the walls that have marks on them in any room. With today's modern latex paints and washable equipment, it only takes an hour or so per room.

Dust and clean blinds, closets (including shelves), windowsills and baseboards. Dry-clean the draperies.

Kitchen

This is a vital area. If it's clean, prospective tenants will feel the whole house is clean (assuming you've haven't left a mess in the bathrooms, as did Hal).

Be sure to clean the oven(s) thoroughly, especially any see-through windows. If you have an electric range, don't waste time cleaning the "spill catchers" under the heating units. Just replace them. They only cost a few dollars each and are readily available at most hardware or grocery stores. And don't forget to clean the stove hood.

Thoroughly clean the sink, dishwasher and any other appliances. Be sure to wash down the walls (assuming they have washable *gloss* paint), and wash and wax the floors.

Be wary of any bad odors or lingering smells. Use of a pine oil cleaning agent and air freshener will usually take care of such problems.

Baths

Clean the tub/shower, sink and toilet. Clean around the base of the toilet as well. Wash the walls (assuming they have washable *gloss* paint), and wash and wax the floors.

As with the kitchen, be wary of any bad odors or lingering smells. Again, use of a pine oil cleaning agent and air freshener will usually take care of such problems.

If that seems like a lot, it is. Assuming that the tenant leaves the property relatively clean, you could still have a few good days of cleaning ahead of you.

Landlord's Rule #20 _____

A clean house attracts a clean tenant.

Hire a Cleaning Service

You don't like cleaning? I don't blame you; neither do I. In the old days (decades ago), I used to do the cleaning myself on all my rentals. However, in recent years I've found that it just doesn't pay. For $100 or so, I can usually get a service that will come in and often in half a day, clean the entire unit far better than I can myself.

Are you worried about the extra cost? I build it into the monthly rental. I set aside $10 a month from the rent for one year and then use it to hire the cleaning service. Even if I had to pay for it out of my pocket, it's worth it to me not to feel that I'm a maid to my tenants.

Don'ts

There are also a number of things that you don't want to do. Those that follow will help you avoid wasting time and money on work that isn't necessary.

Don't Wash Walls, Except in Kitchens and Baths

Today most residential rooms (with the exception of kitchens and baths) are painted with a flat white latex paint. If you go to the store and look at a can, it almost always says "washable." Don't believe it for a minute.

What happens is that over time walls get both uniformly dirty and marked in certain spots. When you look at a wall that hasn't been painted in a year or so, you will see the marks, scratches, stains and so forth. But you won't see the overall dirt. Since it's everywhere, it doesn't stand out.

Just try to wash down the marks or spots on a wall painted in flat latex and you'll see more dirt than when you started. What happens is that where you washed is clean, while everywhere else now looks especially dirty. The overall dirt shows up by comparison. (This isn't usually the case with kitchen or bath walls, which are usually small and use high-gloss paint. The dirt tends to come off these walls uniformly with just a sponge and mild detergent.)

Thus, unless you plan to carefully wash bedroom, living room or dining room walls from floor to ceiling, any washing at all will only make matters worse. That's why I suggest never washing. You should always paint walls—and these days, it's cheap.

Don't Overscrub

I once hired a cleaning person who came in and was so determined to get the kitchen sink clean that she actually scrubbed through the porcelain! You want the property to look clean, but not as sterile as an operating room.

Don't Install New When Old Will Do

There may be rust marks in the dishwasher tray. Replace the tray but not the dishwasher. The tiles in the sink may have a few cracks. Clean and regrout them, but don't replace them. If the carpet has soiled areas and is worn in some walkways, shampoo and use cleaners. Consider a runner to cover the heavily trafficked areas. And if the faucet leaks, put in a new washer—not a new faucet.

What you want to end up with is a property that's clean, tidy, serviceable and profitable. Don't sink your profits into unnecessary repairs. Remember, the tenant is only renting the property, not buying it.

Don't Keep Outmoded Features

In bathrooms, sinks are important. You can replace a stand-alone or wall-hanging sink that looks old-fashioned and cheap with a modern cabinet and sink top for under $200. It will make the bathroom look brighter and more modern, and this will attract a better class of tenant.

An ancient chandelier hanging in the dining room can date a rental. A new, inexpensive one can modernize it.

Old, dark paneling can be depressing and steer potential tenants away. Replacing it with modern, light paneling or even painting over the dark wood can make a big difference.

You get the idea. Many old-fashioned features can be quickly, easily and inexpensively replaced. This will give your rental a much more appealing look.

When To Show the Property

A great rule to remember is that tenants have no imagination. If they see a dirty property, they'll always think of it as dirty. Thus, if you show your rental before you clean it up, you could actually be driving away good tenants.

I prefer to wait until I have my rentals cleaned up before showing them. If someone absolutely has to see a rental, I will show it during the cleaning process. I always avoid showing the rental dirty.

Yes, this may lose me a few days of showing time. But, on the other hand, I usually end up with a better tenant who thinks of the rental as a good place to keep clean.

9

◆◆◆◆◆◆◆

Qualifying the Tenant

The very best way to avoid tenants who pay late, ruin your property or need to be evicted is to not rent to them in the first place. Indeed, the cure for the bad tenant is the good tenant. Rent to the right person, and you simply won't have any problems. The big question of course is, how do you separate the good tenant from the one who will cause you problems?

A Word about Discrimination

In the old days (a long time ago) you as a landlord could rent to anyone you wanted to for any reason at all. The corollary was that you could refuse to rent for any reason at all. Times change and, quite frankly, for the better. Today we have antidiscrimination laws in housing. When you think about it, these laws protect all of us.

For the landlord, however, the news is that you have to watch yourself carefully to be sure that you don't discriminate, even inadvertently. The penalties for discrimination can be severe.

According to the Fair Housing Act, there are a variety of protected classes against which you cannot discriminate in housing. Thus, you cannot discriminate on the basis of any of the following:

- Race or color

- National origin or ancestry

- Religion

- Sex

- Familial status (including children under the age of 18 living with parents or legal custodians and pregnant women and people securing custody of children under the age of 18)

- Physical disability

This is federal law and applies everywhere in the country, including where you have your rental. It means you *cannot* take the following actions based on race, color, national origin, religion, sex, familial status or handicap:

- Refuse to rent housing

- Refuse to negotiate for housing

- Make housing unavailable

- Deny a dwelling

- Set different terms, conditions or privileges for rental of a dwelling

- Provide different housing services or facilities

- Falsely deny that housing is available for inspection or rental

- For profit, persuade owners to rent or deny anyone access to or membership in a facility or service related to the rental of housing

Additionally, if you have a no-pets policy, you must allow a visually impaired tenant to keep a guide dog. If you offer ample, unassigned parking, you must honor a request from a mobility-impaired tenant for a reserved space near his or her apartment, if necessary, to ensure access to the apartment.

And if your tenant has a physical or mental disability (including hearing, mobility and visual impairments; chronic alcoholism; chronic mental illness; AIDS or AIDS-related complex; and mental retardation) that substantially limits one or more major life activities, or has a record of or is regarded as having such disability, you cannot refuse to allow the tenant to make reasonable modification to your dwelling or common-use areas, at the tenant's expense, if necessary for the handicapped person to use the housing. You cannot refuse to make reasonable accommodations in rules, policies, practices or services for a handicapped person to use the housing.

If you refuse to accommodate the injured person, he or she can file a complaint with the Department of Housing and Urban Development (HUD), and you could be subject to an investigation and, potentially, severe fines. If you have any questions, you can call the Fair Housing Clearinghouse operated by HUD. They have free brochures as well as books for sale that explain the law in detail. Their number is 1-800-343-3442.

In addition, local areas may create ordinances that add new classes to the list. You should check with your local housing authority or a knowledgeable real estate agent who specializes in rentals in your area to find out if there are new ordinances. Some that have been passed include the following:

- *Educational status.* You can't discriminate because an applicant is a student.

- *Sexual preference.* You can't discriminate if the applicants are homosexual.

- *Occupation.* You can't discriminate on the basis of what the applicant does for a living.

- *Medical status.* You can't discriminate on the basis of the applicant's medical condition (e.g., if the applicant has AIDs).

- *Age.* You can't discriminate based on age.

Finally, there also are ordinances that have been passed by some local governments that add special restrictions. Here are some that have recently been passed by a few communities in southern California:

- *Number of occupants per house.* You cannot rent to more than four adults (over 18 years of age) per single-family unit.

- *Number of cars.* Tenants cannot have more than two cars per rental unit.

◆

Landlord's Dilemma

With so many antidiscrimination laws on the books, how do you keep out the bad tenants (those who won't pay or might ruin your property) and get the good ones?

The good news is that you are free to discriminate in those areas that are critical to getting a good tenant. Namely, you can reject a tenant who has a bad rental record (e.g., evictions, late payments, bad credit, etc.), who doesn't have enough income to make the payments, who doesn't have enough cash to move in, who has too many members in the family for the size of the property, who has a pet that would damage the property and so on.

In other words, you can still go after the good tenants—i.e., those who make the rent payments on time and keep the place in good shape.

How Many Is Too Many?

One area worth a special note has to do with the number of tenants you allow in your property. Federal law emphasizes that you can't discriminate by refusing to rent to families. On the other hand, local statutes might require that you limit the number of people you can have in your property. What are you to do?

The problem is that there are no hard and fast rules. Building and safety codes usually only state the maximum number of occupants per room, and frequently that's as many as a dozen! Unless local codes specify the maximum you can have in your house, you have to come up with some reasonable rules of your own and *apply them across the board.* As long as you don't change them for each tenant applicant and they're reasonable, you will probably be okay.

Renting to Families with Kids

A word about children is also in order. The old maxim that landlords used to live by was, "Kids are great in your place, not mine!" The reason is that kids are hard on a rental. They tend to mark walls, stain carpets, scratch floors and doors and so on. Many landlords simply prefer to rent to couples without children.

While you can no longer discriminate against a family because it has children, you can limit the number of children you will allow based on the size of the rental. The fewer kids in the rental, of course, the less damage is likely to occur.

So how many children should you allow per rental? As noted earlier, this is a gray area. Some landlords arbitrarily use the guideline of a maximum of two per bedroom. On the other hand, if you have a five-bedroom house, would you want a family with two adults and eight kids living there? There also are other considerations such as how many bathrooms, the total living space, the yard and so on.

As noted earlier, you will want to make any limitations you impose reasonable. And you will want to apply them across the board.

Note: There are certain "adults only" communities where any resident must be, for example, over 55 years of age. Generally speaking, these situations are allowed if all occupants (or in some cases at least 80 percent) meet this requirement.

Giving Out the Rental Application

By the time you meet a would-be tenant at your property, you should have prequalified him or her over the phone. Your job now, as noted in Chapter 8, is to sell the unit. Once you've done that and the tenant is ready to rent, you need to give him or her a rental application.

◆ **CAUTION**   Offer everyone who comes to see the property a rental application, even if they don't seem interested. You don't want to be accused of discrimination by refusing to give out an application.

Choosing a Rental Application

There is no one rental application that is the best, nor do you need to pay a lawyer to create one for you. Perfectly good rental application forms are available at many stationery stores. You want a form that asks the right questions. With the help of modern computers and word processors, you can even create your own application in a short time. The application in Figure 9.1 covers the essential areas you need information on.

As you can see from Figure 9.1, the information requested is extensive but not too extensive. There's nothing on the form that the prospective tenant shouldn't be able to answer in five or ten minutes of writing, perhaps right at the rental site. In other words, though the form is long, it's easy to fill out and only requests information that should be readily available. I don't know of any legitimate reason why a tenant should refuse to fill it out for you. *Note:* Be sure the would-be tenant fills the form out *completely*, especially the section on former landlords.

Make No Promises You Can't Keep

The application is not just a formality. Never, ever rent to anyone without first verifying the information on the form, no matter how perfect they seem. And never tell anyone that the rental is theirs to have before you've finished checking them out. Later, if there's a problem and you don't want to rent to them, they can complain that you're discriminating because first you agreed to rent to them and now you are refusing.

Also, sometimes there will be two or maybe even three would-be tenants at the rental property at the same time, all asking for applications. Don't imply that the first person with the application back gets the prize. You want to rent to the most qualified tenant, not the fastest writer.

Landlord's Rule #21

Never rent to anyone who doesn't fill out an application. Never rent before checking out the application. Do a good job when you check out the tenant.

Five Critical Tenant Tests

Getting a completed rental application is only the first step. Now you must check on what the tenant says. At this point, we could go over the

FIGURE 9.1 Rental Application Form

CAVEAT *Portions of the following form may not apply to your circumstances or may not even be legal in your state or area.* **Do not use it or any prewritten form as it is.** *Take it to a competent attorney in your area so that it may be customized for your state and locale and for your particular needs. The author and publisher assume no responsibility for the legality, appropriateness or timeliness of this form.*

APPLICANT(S)

PROPERTY ADDRESS: 1820 Morgan Place, Los Angeles, CA

APPLICANT'S NAME: Peter Miller

SOCIAL SECURITY NO.: 123-456-7890 DRIVERS LIC. NO.: A123456789

COAPPLICANT: Dorothy Miller

SOCIAL SECURITY NO.: 098-765-4321 DRIVERS LIC. NO.: A987654321

NAME AND RELATIONSHIPS OF OTHER OCCUPANTS:

Daughter Sandra Miller   AGE: 11
Son   Peter Jr. Miller AGE: 7

PETS: Dog, Cocker

AUTOS: 2   MAKE: Buick   MODEL: 4-Door   LICENSE NO.: 123ABC

MAKE: Dodge   MODEL: Coupe   LICENSE NO.: 234ABC

HOUSING INFORMATION

CURRENT ADDRESS: 23 Maple Lane, Ventura, CA

YEARS: 1 MOS: 3 REASON FOR LEAVING: Want bigger place

CURRENT PHONE NO.: 555-9754

CURRENT LANDLORD/MANAGER: James T. Jones PHONE: 555-8887

PREVIOUS ADDRESS: 1429 Smith Lane, Santa Clara, CA

PREVIOUS LANDLORD/MANAGER: Peter Smith PHONE: 555-1122

YEARS: 2 MOS: 6 REASON FOR LEAVING: Want bigger place

FIGURE 9.1 (Continued)

EMPLOYMENT

EMPLOYER: HardHats Ltd. OCCUPATION: Welder

 YEARS: 3 SUPERVISOR: Mr. Smith PHONE: 555-9987

PREVIOUS EMPLOYER: Jimmy's Welding OCCUPATION: Welder

 YEARS: 1 SUPERVISOR: Jimmy Smith PHONE: 555-4322

SPOUSE'S EMPLOYER: OceanView School Dist.

OCCUPATION: Teacher

 YEARS: 4 SUPERVISOR: Mr. Jones PHONE: 555-2235

INCOME AND SAVINGS

MONTHLY GROSS INCOME: $2,430

SPOUSE'S MONTHLY GROSS: $1,320

OTHER INCOME: $ —

CHECKING ACCNT.: First Bank BRANCH: Arroyo St.

   #5545665 LENGTH: 3 Yrs.

SAVINGS ACCNT.: First Bank BRANCH: Arroyo St.

   #H47855 LENGTH: 3 Yrs.

REFERENCES

PERSONAL REFERENCE: Henry Miller

   RELATIONSHIP: Father   PHONE: 555-8475

PERSONAL REFERENCE: George Jones

   RELATIONSHIP: Neighbor   PHONE: 555-5665

IN AN EMERGENCY CONTACT: Jane Brown

   RELATIONSHIP: Mother   PHONE: 555-2203

MAJOR CREDIT CARD: Visa No.:123456789 BAL.: $875

MAJOR CREDIT CARD: Standard Oil No.:23456789 BAL.: $100

FIGURE 9.1   Rental Application Form (Continued)

CREDIT REFERENCE: Al's Pizza PHONE: 555-3323

HOW MANY PEOPLE WILL OCCUPY THIS RENTAL UNIT? 4

NAMES OF OTHER OCCUPANTS: Given

HAVE YOU EVER BEEN EVICTED? No

HAVE YOU EVER FILED BANKRUPTCY? No

I HAVE READ THIS ENTIRE APPLICATION, AND ALL OF THE INFORMA-
TION I HAVE GIVEN IS TRUE AND CORRECT. I HEREBY GIVEN PERMIS-
SION TO LANDLORD TO VERIFY ABOVE INFORMATION, INCLUDING A
CREDIT CHECK.

DATE: 12/5/94

SIGNED BY APPLICANT: Peter Miller

SIGNED BY COAPPLICANT: Dorothy Miller

---

form line by line. However, we're going to cut to the chase and go over
the five critical tests that determine if a tenant is a good prospect. If the
would-be tenant fails any of these five tests, don't rent to them.

Test #1: Does the Landlord before the Current One Recommend the Tenant?

This is the most critical test of all. You're asking an opinion of the
person who is in the best position to know about this tenant. Note that
the application form asks for the name, address and phone number not
only of their current landlord but of the previous landlord. I wouldn't
waste my time checking out the current landlord. If your would-be
tenants are a problem, the current landlord will tell you they are wonderful, just so he or she can get rid of them! Only the landlord before the
present one is likely to give you a true picture.

Test #2: Will the Tenant Give Up His or Her Pet?

As landlords know, pets can take a high toll on a rental. They can scratch, tear, urinate and defecate on the property, all of which can cause thousands of dollars of damage. (One cat urinating on a carpet can destroy that carpet, the padding and even the flooring underneath!)

Ideally, you should rent without pets. However, in the real world you must assume that many, if not most, tenants will have pets. Therefore, the only question is, how many and what kind?

◆

Pets Are a Reality

Hal simply refused to rent to anyone who had a pet. He figured it was the easiest way to go. Consequently, as soon as would-be tenants learned about this, they told him they didn't have any pets. However, almost invariably, a few weeks or a month after they moved in, a pet (or two) would appear.

As soon as Hal found out, he would go over to the property, shout at the tenants and tell them to get rid of the pet or leave. Likely as not, the tenants would get angry and after a few months, depart, often leaving the property a mess.

As a result, Hal lost a lot of rental time and spent a lot of money cleaning up his properties. No, he didn't have any pets, but he didn't have many tenants either.

My suggestion is that you learn to live with the fact that tenants tend to have pets. Otherwise, be prepared to do a lot of shouting and evicting.

Once you come to accept pets, the real issue is one of controlling the number, the kind and their deportment. The first two issues are a function of the rental application; the last is a function of the deposit. (A bigger deposit because of a pet often ensures that the owners take special care to see that the pet is properly behaved.)

After filling out the line on the application about pets, many would-be tenants will ask if you accept them. You can say something such as, "Yes, provided it's a small pet and only a dog (or cat or goldfish or whatever)." At this point the tenant may say something such as, "But I have three

Doberman Pinschers. They are wonderful dogs—and so well behaved and clean."

They certainly may be. But it's doubtful they would have room in a studio apartment with no yard. In fact, it might even be cruel to keep them in such close quarters. When you explain this to the tenant, he or she may say, "It's a shame. But I want this place. Okay, I'll get rid of them." At this point, I have a good friend, a property manager for more than 25 years, who says, "I'm sorry, but I would never rent to anyone who would get rid of a pet!"

The point, of course, is that pets are like members of the family. Almost no one will give them up. If they say they will, they are probably fabricating. Rent to this person and within a few weeks or months, the pet(s) will probably be living there, too.

Test #3: Can the Tenant Come Up with the Cash?

These days it can take a fair amount of cash to move into a rental. Let's say you are renting for $875 a month. Of course, you will want the first month's rent up front. But you will also want a security/cleaning deposit. It wouldn't be unusual to ask for a cleaning deposit equal to a month's rent, or another $875. Now the would-be tenant has to come up with $1,750. (If you're also looking for a lease with first and last month's rent, that's another $875, so the tenant now needs $2,625—sometimes an impossible amount.) That's a fair bit of change for a tenant who is interested in renting a place for under $900 a month.

I always insist that this money must be paid before a tenant can move in. Sometimes tenants will try to negotiate. They may say they'll pay the first month's rent right now, but they would like to pay the security/cleaning deposit in two or three installments over the next few weeks. They just can't come up with all the necessary cash.

It's a believable explanation, and in a tight market you will be tempted to accept it. Just ask yourself, however, what's the point of having a security/cleaning deposit that you can't collect immediately? Furthermore, my experience is that a tenant who can't come up with the money initially will have trouble coming up with it later on as well.

Landlord's Rule #22 _____

Get the cash.

_____

The tenant should pay the first month's rent plus security deposit (plus last month's rent, if applicable) in the form of cash, cashier's check or money order. I will accept a personal check with the understanding that the tenant won't move in until it clears my bank, usually two or three days.

Test #4: Does the Tenant Have Sufficient Income To Make the Payments?

This is like qualifying a person for a home mortgage. The rental application form asks for the prospective tenant's income. According to many property management authorities, you should be sure that the tenant's gross income is at least four or five times the monthly rent. That supposedly ensures that they have enough money coming in to handle the rent. These authorities even have formulas for income, expenses, bank savings and so on that you can apply to a tenant to determine whether or not they will be able to make their monthly payments.

In my experience, however, that's a lot of bunk. I've rented to tenants who had no apparent income yet managed just fine with the rent. And I've rented to tenants who showed more than five times the monthly rent in income yet still couldn't make the rent payments.

To properly qualify a tenant for financial ability to pay, you need to know not only their gross income but the taxes they pay, their monthly fixed expenses, any long-term debt (over six months, such as car payments), any personal debt (such as alimony) and on and on. Quite frankly, you're not likely to get that kind of information on most rental application forms. (And even if you do, it still won't *prove* anything. Mortgage lenders use very fine pencils, and a percentage of their loans still go bad.)

Therefore, instead of using a sharp pencil and some arcane formula, sit down with the rental application form and the prospective tenant to whom you want to rent the property and ask, "Do you figure you'll be able to handle the monthly rent payments? Where will you get the money?"

Tenants usually consider this a reasonable question from a prospective landlord, and those who have their act together will often quickly outline their basic expenses (including utilities, food and so on), their fixed expenses and their income to prove to me that it will work. I really don't pay much attention to the proof; the fact that they have a plan is usually enough. I just want to be sure that they know where the rent money is coming from and are confident they can find it. (I also check with their employer and bank to be sure they aren't making money up out of thin air.)

Note: To be in compliance with antidiscrimination laws you will need to be sure to ask the same questions and apply the same criteria to all tenants.

◆

Even Unemployed People Can Pay Their Rent

I once had a would-be tenant who said he was currently unemployed—in fact, had been unemployed for the past 18 months. He had no regular income.

I naturally was concerned and asked how he expected to make the rent payments. He proceeded to inform me that the reason he was unemployed was that he had been injured at work and had received a cash settlement of over $200,000, which he had banked. He was happy to have me confirm this with his bank. He said he planned on living on the money for a year or two before getting a new job.

I rented to him, and he stayed two years, paying in cash right on the due date.

Verifications.   If a tenant says he or she doesn't have much income but does have a lot of cash in the bank, don't hesitate to confirm that with a bank. Have the tenant sign a standard verification of deposit request and send it off to the bank.

If the tenant says they are depending on income from their employment to make the rent payments, be sure the credit check you do (discussed in Test #5) confirms their employment. If it doesn't, then use your own verification of employment form. (See Figure 9.2.)

Test #5: Does the Tenant Have a Good Credit and Rental History?

I consider this the second most important factor in qualifying a tenant. You must have some idea of how they handle bills, and about the only way you ascertain this is through an independent credit and/or rental history check. (*Note:* Your rental application should provide that the tenant gives you permission to make such a check.)

FIGURE 9.2 Request To Verify Employment

(Name)

(Company)

(Address)

(Date)

Dear Employer:

_____(*tenant's name*) has applied to rent a house (*apt./condo*) from me and has given you as his/her (*select one*) employer. He/she (*select one*) says that he/she has worked for you for the past _____ years/months at a weekly salary of $_____.

I would very much appreciate it if you would verify this for me so that I can proceed with qualifying _____ (*tenant's name*) for the rental. Please call me as soon as possible at _____.
If you are unable to call, please fill out the area below and return this sheet to me.

Sincerely,

 Landlord
_____

_____

[ ] Verified as given [ ] Temporary [ ] Permanent [ ] Not verified

Comments: _____

Employer: _____

Many landlords feel that getting a credit report is a hassle and requires too much time. I don't. It may be confusing the first time, but after you've established a method for getting a credit report, it should be easy to do. Besides, the information it provides can be invaluable.

Sally Discovers the Importance of Credit Checks

Sally had never used a credit reporting agency for her tenants and had had fairly good luck. She would call the previous and current landlords, check with the tenant's employer and bank and let it go at that. But finally she decided to go with a credit report.

Imagine her surprise when the very first check she ran revealed that the prospective tenant had dozens of late payment and defaulted accounts. The would-be tenant's application looked perfect. Her employer verified her employment. The bank said she had enough money on deposit to move in. But the credit report revealed she was a true deadbeat.

Needless to say, Sally now uses credit checks on all her prospective tenants.

The question is, how do you as a single landlord run a credit check and rental history check?

Credit Checks. There are numerous credit-checking agencies in every metropolitan area (listed under "credit reporting agencies" in the yellow pages) in addition to the three national credit agencies—Equifax, TRW and TransUnion. A formal, written credit report from one of the major agencies, however, usually costs anywhere from $35 to $50 and thus usually is prohibitively expensive for rental credit checks.

However, many local agencies have a special single-service option designed just for landlords where for a much smaller fee, often only $10 or $20, they will do a minimal credit search. Sometimes they only report back verbally, and in other cases they issue you a minimal written credit report.

Sometimes, really good tenants will have already pulled their own credit report and will bring it to you. And sometimes, real estate brokers or lawyers can get one for you from an online computer service.

Finally, many areas have rental or landlord associations that belong to a credit reporting agency and can run a check for you at a nominal cost.

Note: You can ask the prospective tenant to pay all or a portion of the cost of the credit report. Some would-be tenants will balk at this, while others will feel it's perfectly natural, particularly if the cost is only around $10 or $15. I only ask for the tenant to pay for the report if the rental market is really tight and there are far more tenants than rentals. The rest of the time, I pay for it myself. After all, I'm only going to get a credit report on a tenant whom I'm pretty sure I want.

Rental History Check.   What can be even more revealing than a credit check is a rental history check. Today there are landlord associations in virtually all metropolitan areas. (Look under "landlord associations" or "housing associations" in the yellow pages.)

These associations receive reports of late payments and evictions from their members and then make the information available. Sometimes you will have to join the organization to get a rental history check (which could be quite expensive with annual dues), but other times the association will make it available to you for a nominal fee, as long as you agree to provide information on tenants to them. In other words, they'll scratch your back if you scratch theirs.

Sometimes these associations are tied in to others across the state and even between states.

If a prospective tenant shows up with a bad report on a rental history check, I would be very careful about renting to him or her. No matter what explanations are given, what a tenant did to one landlord they are likely to do to another.

If the tenant passes the five tests, then I feel I've got a winner and will rent to him or her.

Agreeing on a Move-in Date

Once you've got a tenant whom you feel is qualified, call them back and say you're willing to rent to them, provided both of you can come to an agreement on a few areas. One of the most important of these areas is the move-in date.

Tenants will always want to move in at a time that's most convenient for them. And of course they want the rent to start when they move in, not before. This, however, can cost you money. For example, let's say that your property is available on the 1st of the month. However, you don't find a tenant until the 15th. You've qualified the tenant and are ready to have them sign a rental agreement. They are willing to sign and give you a check for all monies. However, they can't move in until the 1st of the next month and want the rent to start as of then.

If you allow the rent to start on the 1st, you will have lost another two weeks of income. I always tell these tenants that the property is now available and I can't lose two weeks rent waiting for them. They can move in on the 1st if they choose, but the rent must start on the 15th.

What usually happens is that there's a discussion and the tenant comes back with an offer to compromise. They suggest splitting the difference. The rent can start one week before the 1st. I lose a week and they lose one as well. If it's a strong tenant in a weak market, I'm willing to compromise. After all, it will probably take me another two weeks to find another suitable applicant.

What I usually do is make a counteroffer. The rent will start one week before the 1st. However, the following month, the tenants will pay five weeks rent instead of four. That will move their payment date up to the 1st. It's always to your advantage to have the payment date on the 1st. Most tenants will agree to this compromise and be satisfied with it.

The Next Step

After we finish negotiating, I have the prospective tenants sign a lease or month-to-month agreement (discussed in Chapter 10); once they are signed up, I have a walk-through (discussed in Chapter 12).

To get started, obtain a rental application, make sure the tenant checks out and you're on your way!

10

••••◆•••

Writing the Rental Agreement

Most people would concede that the most important document in landlord-tenant relations is the rental agreement. After all, it spells out in writing just what that relationship actually is (subject, of course, to local, state and federal laws). Armed with a strong rental agreement, you will have a much better time dealing with your tenants. For one thing, they will know exactly what you expect. For another, if push comes to shove and you end up in small-claims court, a good agreement will help you to prevail.

Rental agreements are abundantly available. Call up almost any real estate agent, and they can provide you with an agreement, often on a complimentary basis. It's part of the good will they do in the hopes that eventually you will sell your property through them. A wide variety of companies publish rental agreements and sell them in stationery stores, through bookstores that have real estate sections and sometimes even through REALTOR® boards. Some state departments of real estate also have suggested forms. Of course, you can always go to a lawyer and have an agreement drawn up from scratch, specifically for your own needs.

After you've looked at many different rental agreements, you'll begin to see that they all have about the same sort of boilerplate in them and refer to the same sort of potential problems. Most property managers I know start out with a published form and then add to it, adapting the agreement to their own needs. This usually works very well for them. I have provided my own sample, which appears in Appendix A.

◆ **CAUTION**   The rental agreement in the Appendix and clauses I suggest in this chapter are those that work for me. But they may not work for you. Keep in mind that real estate rules and laws are different from state to state and even within local areas within states. As a result, just because these forms work for me does not mean they are appropriate everywhere. They may not be suitable for your area. There may be clauses that are illegal in your state or locale. The wording may not even be acceptable to a court in your area.

Therefore, my suggestion is that you do *not* use any agreement unless you first take it to your own attorney to have it adapted to your specific locale and usage. Yes, that might cost you a few bucks, but it could save you a lot of money down the road. (Of course, you could always go out and buy one of the prepared forms for your area in a stationery store, but you'd be best off having an attorney check that over as well.)

Month-to-Month Agreement versus Lease

The first thing you will discover is that there are two types of rental agreements: (1) month-to-month tenancy and (2) a lease. (Actually, the two types technically used are oral and written, but these days a landlord would be a fool, in my opinion, to use anything but a written agreement.) There are proponents of both month-to-month and leases. Keep in mind that the type you choose will have important ramifications on your relationship with your tenants.

The basic difference between the two types of rental agreements is that the month-to-month agreement is for an *indeterminate* period of time. Once begun, the agreement typically continues in force until cancelled, usually by 30 days' notice from either party (the time can vary depending on the state). The lease, on the other hand, is for a very *specific* period of time, most commonly one year, although it could be for longer or less time.

Most new landlords immediately seize upon the lease as the best document to use. The reason is that it ties up the tenant for a specific period of time (as noted, often a year) so that the landlord presumably doesn't have to worry about rerenting the property. They anticipate signing the lease and then forgetting about it.

Unfortunately, that's not always the way it works out. With leases, there can often be a big difference between the way things are supposed to work and the way they actually do work out.

Concerns with Leases

There are a number of concerns with leases that experienced property managers often express. These usually lead them back to the month-to-month tenancy as not wonderful but preferable. Let's look at some of these concerns.

Inability To Raise Rents

Not only does the lease lock in the tenants for a specific period of time, but it also locks in the landlord. For example, if during the lease period the market tightens up and you discover that rentals similar to yours have increased $50 to $100 in rate, you can't increase your rates, short of breaking the lease. The lease specifies not only the amount to be paid each month but the total amount to be paid over the life of the lease. You're locked in. This is particularly of concern with longer-term leases—those of a year or more.

Furthermore, if during the term of the lease you decide to sell the property, you can't kick the tenants out so the new owner can move in. The tenants have rights to the property until at least the last day of the lease. In order to get them to agree to move out, you might have to offer some inducement, such as a giving them six months' worth of rent. You're the one who is locked in.

But, of course, new landlords will point out that the tenants are locked in as well. That's technically true, but for practical purposes, the tenants are only locked in to the degree that they want to be locked in.

Tenants Aren't Really Locked In

For example, let's say you have a two-year lease with a tenant for a house, and after three months the tenant loses his or her job and can't work. He or she may very well be able to break the lease on the grounds that he or she no longer has access to the money he or she was anticipating when the lease was made.

Maybe the tenant entered military service during the course of the lease. That could be sufficient grounds for breaking it.

Furthermore, what if the tenants don't have a good reason for breaking the lease but simply up and move out. What are you going to do then?

Normally your only recourse is to sue for the rent, usually as it comes due. The problem is that the tenants may be hard to find. They may leave the city or even the state, and tracking them down can be costly. Furthermore, even if you find them, they may be judgment-proof—i.e., they may have no assets that you can easily attach. Finally, you have a duty to mitigate damages—i.e., you have a responsibility to try to rerent the property while you're out there trying to track down the tenants. This is not only a legal but a logical thing to do. After all, why leave the property vacant when it can be producing rent? The problem is that the money you receive in rent must usually be subtracted from the amount you can claim from your tenant who moved out.

In short, what usually happens with a tenant who skips on a lease is that the landlord quickly rerents the property and then turns the matter over to a collection agency, hoping that sometime in the future he or she may get some money back. As often as not, nothing comes in.

Landlord's Rule #23

A lease locks in only those who have some assets and who want to be locked in.

On the other hand, let's say that you want to break the lease and get the tenant out, but the tenant is unwilling. Your recourse may be to go to court. In a situation like this you better have an ironclad reason for wanting the tenant out and an attorney as good as Perry Mason.

By the way, you can sell your property even if you have a lease on it. If you sell a property with a lease on it, the new owner normally takes over subject to the lease. That is, the new owner inherits the old tenant and the old lease. The biggest problem here usually involves the cleaning/security deposit. The new owner is probably responsible for paying it back when the tenant moves out (assuming the property is left clean), although the old owner may be responsible for notifying the tenants. But in many states the old owner may keep the money unless a provision that it be transferred over is specified as part of the sale. In fact, as noted in Chapter 20, handling the cleaning/security deposit money is one of the more important elements in the sale of a property with a lease on it.

A Lease May Preclude Getting a Cleaning/Security Deposit

Finally, the one practical reason that property managers cite the most for not wanting to use a lease is that it may preclude your getting a substantial cleaning/security deposit. The reasoning here is really quite simple.

In a lease the landlord typically asks for first and last month's rent. Let's say you're renting a property for $750 a month. Double that figure (first and last month's rent), and the tenant now must come up with $1,500 in rent money before moving in. True, what you're asking is nothing more than paying the last month's rent first—i.e., when that last month rolls around, the tenant won't have to pay anything. But do you know anyone these days who has a lot of cash sitting around unused?

Now add on top of this $1,500 a cleaning deposit, which might be another $700 dollars or so, and the move-in costs rise to over $2,200. In a tight rental market where there are many tenants chasing few properties, you might indeed get this much. But in a more normal market where landlords are in competition for a limited supply of tenants, you probably won't. Before coming up with all that money for you, a tenant is more likely to go to your competition who charges less.

As a result, most landlords who insist on a lease end up getting no cleaning/security deposit or more likely, a smaller one. They may, for example, accept only a few hundred dollars as the deposit.

The mistake that these landlords make, in my opinion, is to think that the last month's rent is better than the cleaning/security deposit. Remember, you can't apply the last month's rent to cleaning. You can only apply it to rent. But the cleaning/security deposit often can be applied either to unpaid rent or to cleaning.

◆

Sally's Mountain Rental Turns into a Disaster

Sally purchased a mountain rental home and found tenants who were willing to rent it for $750 a month. The tenants, however, were quite savvy and insisted on a lease, offering Sally first and last month's rent plus a $100 cleaning deposit. Sally was eager to rent since the property was several hours by car from where she lived and showing it was a real hassle. So she accepted the offer.

The tenants stayed the entire lease period, 15 months, and never called once to complain about anything. Their rent was also paid on time, and Sally thanked her lucky stars that she had been so fortunate, particularly since the rental was so far away from her home.

When she came to get the key from the tenants on the day they were to move out, she found they had already left and had trashed her mountain home. Apparently they had used the property for a long series of orgies during which the walls had received stains and holes in them, one toilet had been ripped from the floor and broken, a small fire had taken out part of the kitchen and roof and the grounds had been totally left to go to weed.

Yes, she had the $100 deposit, which the tenants didn't even bother to claim, but they had done thousands in damage, most of which her insurance wouldn't cover. She lost another month and a half in rent getting the property habitable again.

There are three morals here. The first is to always get as big a cleaning/security deposit as possible. The second is to always check up regularly on your rentals, even if you don't hear from your tenants. And the third is never buy a rental far from home.

When the Lease Expires

One point that many landlords fail to realize is that in most states, when a lease expires—i.e., the time period runs out—no *notice* is required from either party of termination. Many leases do provide, however, that if the tenant does *not* move, the tenancy converts to month-to-month and can stay that way indefinitely. After the lease expires and the tenancy converts to month-to-month, to get the tenant out, you must now give notice, usually 30 days. The same applies to the tenants when they want to leave.

Note: Many state laws governing notice in month-to-month tenancy specify 30 days as a *minimum*. But there is no actual maximum. If there's a particular need, I have sometimes agreed to 60 or even 90 days' notice. Tenants might insist on this, for example, if you're planning to sell the property. They want to be sure they have time to find a new property if you sell and ask them to leave.

Hanging Your Hat on a Month-to-Month Tenancy

As indicated, the most popular alternative to the lease is the month-to-month tenancy. This leaves both the landlord and the tenant free to pull the plug upon proper notification. If you want the tenant out, you simply give notice. On the other hand, if the tenants want out, they just give you notice and move.

The Revolving Door Tenancy

The biggest problem with the month-to-month tenancy, however, is its indeterminacy. Most landlords don't want tenants moving in and out as though through a revolving door. No matter how big a deposit or how clean the tenants leave the property, there will always be some cleanup work after each tenant that you will have to do yourself and pay for yourself. There's also the time it takes to rerent—anywhere from a few days to a few weeks or a month or more—during which you lose rent.

A landlord who has one tenant who stays for a year is usually doing far better than a landlord who has three tenants who each stay for four months. Unless you're running a motel or hotel, the last thing you want are itinerant tenants.

Incentives To Stay

Several landlords I know build a kind of incentive into their month-to-month agreements, hoping to get tenants to stay longer. They ask for a somewhat lower cleaning/security deposit and in addition ask for a non-refundable onetime cleaning fee (where allowed by local statute). This fee typically is around $125. The tenant pays it up front and realizes that it won't come back.

However, the landlord then notes that for each month the tenant stays in the property, a portion of the fee will be refunded, perhaps $15 a month. If the tenant stays for nine months, for example, the tenant gets back the full $125.

No, it's not a huge amount of money. But it is something that sticks in tenants' minds. When they think about moving, they are reminded of the cleaning fee, which might be just enough incentive to make them stay.

◆ **CAUTION**   Be careful that the refund doesn't constitute payment for work, or else you might be considered an employer under federal and/or state laws. If you're an employer, many rules and regulations may apply, including withholding, paying Social Security and more. Check with an attorney or a knowledgeable property manager in your area.

The Lease/Month-to-Month Hybrid

Today some property managers are using a kind of hybrid lease and month-to-month combination rental agreement. It won't work in every area or for every rental, but it's good to be aware of this option.

The hybrid is a lease in every way, except that the landlord does not demand that the last month's rent be paid up front. Rather, the tenant only pays the first month's rent and then a large cleaning/security deposit. This gets around the problem of not being able to get a large security deposit with a lease and only being able to use the last month's rent for purposes of rent.

The advantage of this hybrid is that it is for a specific period of time. At least for its psychological advantage, the tenants are made aware that they are expected to stay in the property for the lease's term, perhaps a year or more. On the other hand, the disadvantage is that it does lock in the landlord to that particular tenant at that particular rent.

The Problem with Asking for Attorney's Fees

Historically, at least going back about 30 years, rental agreements tended to include a section that said that if landlord and tenant went to court over enforcement or other provisions of the agreement, the loser would pay the winner's attorney fees.

I suspect the reason behind this clause was twofold. First, it put the tenants on notice that filing frivolous lawsuits against the landlord would be costly. And second, it gave the landlord at least the possibility of collecting the costs of his or her attorney fees after winning the suit. But what if the landlord loses?

Years ago it was a forgone conclusion that unless there was some unusual circumstance, by the time a suit got to court involving a tenancy, the landlord was going to win. Not any longer. Today small-claims courts may actually favor the tenant. Even if you feel you are 100 percent right, you have no guarantee that you will win. (See the movie *Pacific Heights*, available on video tape, to get some idea of how bad things can go.)

Consider the consequences of losing:

- You're out your rent.

- You're out your attorney fees.

- You're probably out cleaning costs.

- And now you're going to have to pay the tenant's attorney fees!

As a result, today many landlords think twice before including a clause on winner paying loser's attorney fees. It's one of those apparently great ideas that could come back to haunt you.

Arbitration Clauses

Some landlords now insert binding arbitration clauses in their leases. If there is a dispute, both parties agree to take it before an arbitrator and abide by the decision.

The trouble is that arbitrators who are specialists and belong to national arbitration associations often charge high fees. Thus, the cost of an arbitrator can be more than the amount in dispute. And getting both landlord and tenant to agree to some other third party as an arbitrator can be difficult.

Avoid Unenforceable Clauses

A rental agreement is a contract that is presumably binding on both parties. But even so, you cannot give up rights that you have under law by signing a contract. For example, perhaps you want to have a clause in your rental agreement that precludes tenants from suing you for injuries they sustain while renting your property. The problem is that it's very hard to preclude someone from suing you. They usually have the right to sue just as they have the right to free speech and the "quiet enjoyment" of your property during the rental period.

Including unenforceable clauses only confuses and clutters up your rental agreement. In addition, they may give the other side more ammunition if push comes to shove and you end up in court.

You also should avoid a lot of legalese in your rental forms, even if you're a lawyer. Make your forms plain so that they can be understood. You don't want your tenants to say they couldn't understand what they were signing.

Creating Your Rental Agreement

As noted earlier, I have included my rental agreement in Appendix A. Remember that it's my form, not yours. Before you use this form, take it to your attorney so he or she can see if it will work for you and can adapt it to the laws in your area as well as your specific needs.

Also keep in mind that your rental agreement should be considered a work in progress. Existing laws and regulations are constantly changing, and new ones are always coming on the books. What works today may not work tomorrow. You need to be prepared to amend this agreement to meet your needs in the future.

11

•••◆•••

How To Handle Deposits

Landlords are always handling deposits of one sort or another. For example, there are the cleaning and security deposits that are almost always part of any tenancy agreement. If a family is interested in renting a property, there may be a deposit to hold the rental for them. Some landlords even insist on a separate deposit for keys (to ensure that they are returned) and another deposit for pets. Some even take a deposit if a tenant has a water bed. Regardless of what the deposit is for, two questions always arise with regard to a deposit. First, how big should it be? And second, what do you do with the money? We'll troubleshoot both concerns in this chapter.

The Purpose of Deposits

The purpose of a deposit is to guarantee by money that the tenant will perform (or not perform) a certain act. With a deposit for a pet, for example, the landlord is hoping that having the tenant put up a sum of money will guarantee that the tenant will make sure that the pet will not damage the property. With a cleaning deposit, the hope is that the deposit will ensure that the tenant will keep the property clean or at least clean it up thoroughly before leaving.

Generally speaking, the bigger the deposit, the greater your security.

When To Collect a Deposit

Deposits are usually collected at the time the tenant signs the rental agreement and pays the first (and last) month's rent. Sometimes a tenant doesn't have all the money to pay both the deposit(s) and the rent. There is nothing wrong with having the tenant pay the first month's rent upon signing the rental agreement with the written understanding that the deposit(s) are to be paid in full when the tenant moves in (which could be several days or even weeks later).

Landlord's Rule #24

Never allow a tenant into a property until you have received *all* the deposits.

Any landlord who allows a tenant to move in, or even just to begin moving belongings into the rental unit, without first having collected all monies up front is asking for trouble. The tenant might never pay you another cent, and you'd then have to go through eviction without the benefit of deposits to help ease the burden.

◆

No Tenant Is Better Than a Bad Tenant

Sally had a small two-bedroom house she was renting out in a bad market where there were too many rentals chasing too few tenants. Her place had been empty for almost two months, and she was getting desperate. She was ready to accept the first person who wanted to rent her unit, and she did.

The new tenants seemed okay, and a credit check showed some problems but nothing catastrophic. However, she couldn't verify their previous rental history because they were from out of the area and said they had always owned their own home before.

The biggest problem was that the new tenants couldn't come up with all the rent money and deposits. But they wanted to move in immediately, on the 15th of the month. They said they would pay two weeks rent in cash. Then, on the 1st, they would pay a full month's rent plus a large cleaning/security deposit. Sally accepted, and they moved in.

But on the 1st they said that the jobs they were expecting to get didn't pan out. They didn't have any money. They were sorry and would move as soon as they could. The soonest they could move turned out to be six weeks later, just as Sally was halfway through eviction proceedings. She not only lost several months rent (including cleanup time) plus some costs, but she also had no deposit to pay for the cleanup of the mess the tenants left.

The moral of this story is that you shouldn't jump from the frying pan into the fire. Remember, having no tenant is better than having a bad tenant.

Always Give a Receipt

Whenever you receive a deposit from a tenant, always give back a receipt. The receipt should state not only the obvious things, such as name, date and amount of the deposit, but should indicate its purpose and under what conditions it will be kept or returned. Never accept a check as a deposit without giving a signed receipt. It's not good business practice.

How Big a Deposit Should You Get?

There is an obvious answer: As big as you can get. However, there are limitations. Tenants will balk at outrageously large deposits; they'll rent from someone else if you charge too much. Also, many states limit the size of the deposit you can take. (Check with your state department of real estate or housing.) For example, the cleaning/security deposit may be limited to one and a half month's rent. (One way you may be able to get around this limitation is to accept several deposits for different purposes—e.g., a cleaning/security deposit and then a separate deposit for a pet. Check with an experienced and knowledgeable property manager in your area.)

The Key to Getting a Large Deposit

The key to getting a large deposit is to make it very clear to the tenant that you intend to return the money, providing that the conditions of the deposit are met. If the pet does no damage, you will promptly return *all* of the deposit. (We'll get into when to return deposits at the end of this chapter.) If the property is left as clean as it was found and you have a method for determining this (see Chapter 12 on the walk-through inspection sheets), you will return all monies. If there is damage, you will subtract the cost, and you have a reasonable method of determining fees.

Once the tenants become convinced that the deposit is not your advance Christmas present, they usually are willing to comply.

Where To Keep the Deposit

Many landlords I know simply put rental deposits in their own personal accounts and spend them immediately as they would other income. There's apparently nothing illegal about this practice in some states, although as a practical matter, it can create some serious problems (in many states, landlords must put deposits in trust accounts that bear interest). First, as soon as you put the money in your own account, you should probably declare it as income for tax purposes. In addition, when the tenant moves out, you need to come up with the deposit money. But what do you do if you've already spent it? Some landlords rob Peter to pay Paul. They quickly rerent the property and use the new tenant's deposit to pay the old—not a good practice.

◆─────────────────────────────────────

Creative Financing Involving Deposits

I have seen some rather amazing real estate transactions take place on the basis of cleaning/security deposits. In one instance the owner of an overpriced, 105-unit apartment building in a very bad market gave the building away (subject to its mortgages, of course) to a buyer, providing she (the original owner) could hang onto the cleaning deposits. Since the average rent of the building was $500 a month and she was holding around 100 deposits equal to one and a half months' rent, she came away with $75,000. Of course, the new owners had to answer to the tenants, who eventually wanted their deposits back.

In another instance a small group of investors took over an empty 500-unit apartment building, borrowing money for the down payment. They then quickly rented it up and used the security deposits they acquired, nearly a half million dollars' worth, to pay back the down payment loan. In essence the deposits helped finance the purchase!

This is not to say you should practice such creative financing. But it does point out the gray area into which deposits fall.

A Separate Bank Account

Most good property managers I know keep their rental deposits in a separate bank account. They have a special record book for keeping track of the deposits, and when tenants move out, the money is readily available to either pay for repairs or pay back the tenants. (Deposit money kept in this fashion may not be considered taxable income. Talk to your tax adviser.)

There are two hidden problems with separate bank accounts that new landlords don't usually appreciate. The first is mundane—namely, how do you create the separate bank account?

You can simply open an account in your name and then refer to it as the "John Smith rental deposit account." Most banks won't bat an eye at setting up the account that way, and checks can be easily deposited to your deposit account. Another method is to set up a trust account. This is more complex, however, because you must keep very accurate records, including for whom you're holding the money in trust. Most real estate agents have these accounts, although some banks may balk at setting them up for individuals.

The trust account gets into some difficulty with regard to the second hidden problem with deposits—interest. If you accept a $1,000 deposit and then put it into a non-interest-bearing account, most people would say you're a fool. On the other hand, if you put the deposit into an interest-bearing account, who gets the interest? You or the tenant whose money you're holding? In some states you can claim the interest for yourself, unless you put the money into an account that is in trust for someone else.

Legislation in some states requires landlords to pay tenants a minimal amount of interest on deposit money. This legislation, however, has been held up in other states, interestingly enough, by falling interest rates. For example, some states, such as Illinois, have stipulated that landlords should pay tenants 5 percent per annum on their money. Today, however, most savings accounts are paying less than 3 percent! Low interest rates have made the whole question moot, and until interest rates rise once again, the legislation is on the back burner in many states.

When To Pay the Deposit Back

As noted elsewhere in this book, most states have passed regulations determining how long a landlord can hold a deposit after a tenant moves out. For example, in California a landlord must pay back the deposit in full or give a complete accounting of how the money was spent within 14 days after a tenant moves out. The time limit varies, so be sure to check in your area.

Most tenants, understandably, don't want to wait 14 days. They may need the money as a deposit on the next place to which they are moving. And they are probably afraid that any delay at all means that the landlord may not return all or most of the money to them. As a consequence, there is a kind of tug-of-war that occurs over the deposit at the time the tenants move out, with some tenants resorting to rather clever tactics to get their deposits back quickly.

A new landlord may ask why he or she shouldn't immediately return all of the deposit as long as the tenant leaves the property clean. "Aha," I can hear experienced landlords saying, "Wait and see! "

The reason has to do with hidden damage that may occur sometime after the tenant moves out. What's hidden damage? In one case of a property I was renting out, the tenant's children had flushed several toys down the drain and plugged it up. But this didn't show up until several days after they moved out, when a cleaning crew was at work in the house. In another case the tenant's pet had left the carpeting infested with fleas. But the tenant had set off a flea bomb, killing all the mature fleas. It wasn't until a week later that the flea eggs hatched, producing a house full of new biting insects and the need to call a pest control company to get rid of them.

It's to the landlord's advantage to hang onto that cleaning deposit as long as possible to ensure that there is money to pay for any hidden damage occuring after the tenant moves out. As noted, however, tenants want that money right away, and some will resort to creative methods to get it.

◆————————————————————

Returning Cleaning Deposits Early Is a Risky Move

Sally owned a three-bedroom house that she rented out to a minister. The man didn't have a great deal of money, but he had excellent credit and his past history of renting was impeccable. He managed to raise the first month's rent and a cleaning deposit almost as large and moved in on a month-to-month tenancy.

After about seven months, the minister called to say things just hadn't worked out with his new church. He was giving three weeks' notice (almost a month) and would be out on the 1st. He would leave the place clean and wanted and expected his cleaning deposit returned on the day he moved out. Sally explained that it would be mailed to him within 14 days. He replied, "We'll see."

On the appointed day, Sally was at the property to receive the key. She had decided to forget the fact that she had received only three weeks' notice instead of a month and went through the property with the minister, conducting the move-out walk-through inspection (described in Chapter 14). The property was generally clean, although there were a few things that needed attention and either the minister said he would fix them immediately or Sally said she would get them done. They agreed to her keeping $35 out of a $1,000 deposit. He then insisted on getting the remaining $965 at once. Sally balked, saying that she would send the money to him within 14 days, provided no other damage appeared. He said he would pay for any damage, but she would have to report it to him and then he would send her a check. He wanted his cleaning deposit, now. She politely refused.

At that point he took her outside to the large mobile home he had parked in the driveway, filled with his belongings. He informed Sally that, God willing, the mobile home with him and his family living in it would move on the day she paid him his cleaning deposit . . . and not a moment sooner.

Sally considered. She could, of course, have taken the matter to court. He couldn't live in a mobile home in her driveway, and they both knew it. But suing would take time (probably more than 14 days), it would be costly and suing a minister was no slam dunk. In the meantime it would be hard to rerent the property with the minister and his family living in the driveway.

She finally said she would give him half the deposit back now and half after two weeks. He was adamant. He wanted it all.

Sally finally gave him a check and waved goodbye as he drove off. As it turned out, she rerented within a few days, and there were no hidden problems.

Problems with Tenant over the Deposit

We've just seen how a tenant creatively handled the matter of getting the cleaning deposit back when he wanted it. There is another technique that tenants use much more frequently, however, and that's using the deposit as the last month's rent.

When the Tenant Uses the Deposit as the Last Month's Rent

As noted in Chapter 10, today most landlords don't use a lease that demands first and last month's rent but instead use a month-to-month rental agreement, securing the first month's rent up front plus a cleaning/security deposit equal to one month's rent. The idea, of course, is that you don't have to automatically pay back the deposit and can instead use it to pay for damages. The last month's rent can only be applied to rent.

Many, dare I say most, tenants, however, would be very pleased to consider the cleaning deposit as the last month's rent. In fact, they may take steps to ensure that it's the last month's rent.

◆

Hal Discovers the Dangers of Applying Cleaning/Security Deposits to Last Month's Rent

Hal rented a flat (one story of a three-story apartment building) to college students for a nine-month period, collecting the first month's rent plus a cleaning/security deposit equal to one month's rent.

The last month was June, the end of the school year, and when Hal went to receive the rent, he was told by the precocious students that they wouldn't pay the last month's rent. Instead, he was free to use the cleaning/security deposit for the rent. Of course, they said they would leave the flat spotless.

Hal didn't like this one bit since it meant that when they moved, he would have no deposit left to cover any lack of cleaning or damage they might have done. He told them he would have them evicted. But the students said that eviction would take a month at the least and would be expensive. Besides, they would be out in 30 days, so why bother? They said that any judge would probably feel the same way.

Hal said he would report them to a landlords' association and a credit report agency. They seemed surprised at his reaction and said he was being mean. However, after talking it over, they said that they were students anyhow, had no assets and didn't care about their credit!

Hal reluctantly gave in. But, when they moved, the place was a mess, and it cost Hal nearly $500 out of pocket to get it in shape for the next tenants.

What could Hal have done to avoid this problem? One answer is to not charge a month's rent as the cleaning/security deposit. If you charge exactly one month's rent, it's too convenient for the tenant to use it as the last month's payment. On the other hand, if you charge slightly less, it makes it harder for the tenant.

For example, let's say the rent is $1,000. Instead of charging $1,000 for the cleaning deposit, why not charge $965? The $35 dollars isn't going to make much difference to you. Yet the different amount makes a big psychological difference when it comes to trading the cleaning/security deposit for the rent.

Another thing to do is to stress the point in big and bold letters in the rental agreement: **This Deposit May Not Be Used for the Last Month's Rent.** It gets the message across more clearly.

Yet another technique is to meet with the tenants *two* months before their planned move and carefully explain to them the consequences of taking such an action. One experienced property manager I know carefully tells tenants that if they try to use the cleaning deposit as the last month's rent, he will feel duty-bound to report them to a credit reporting agency. He also points out that this may affect their future ability to rent or buy another property and even their ability to get future credit, including a credit card. When thus explained beforehand (instead of after the fact, as Hal did in our story), most tenants are less inclined to take rash action.

Finally, it's important to make it perfectly clear to the tenants that you have their cleaning/security deposit safely in hand and that you fully intend and want to return it to them, provided they meet their obligations. If they see that you are honest and well intentioned, they will be less inclined to try to use pressure against you.

Special Problems with Pets

Finally, there's the matter of the deposit for pets. After having been burned many times, my feeling is that the deposit for pets should be very high indeed. As noted earlier, a single cat urinating on a carpet can destroy it, costing you thousands in replacement costs.

It's important to make clear to the tenant that your expectations are that the pet will use the great outdoors for its bathroom or will have a special litter box for use inside. Any damage to the carpet or the house will come out of the cleaning deposit. As you add hundreds of dollars to the pet deposit, you can almost see the deportment of the animal improve.

Note: It's probably a good idea to separate the pet deposit from the cleaning/security deposit. That will emphasize your special concern.

Big Deposits Are Not Always a Guarantee

Hal had a nice house that he rented to a family with two dogs. He got a big, $1,000 pet deposit and felt quite secure.

Several months into the rental, the toilet backed up, flooding the apartment. The reason for the backup was a mystery. The tenant said the toilet had stuck and had kept on flushing, which was apparently true. The plumber said that he thought tree roots had gotten into the line and plugged it. The additional water had then backed up. It was hard to blame the tenant for the problem. Hal immediately had the carpets and padding taken out and sterilized, which had to be done to avoid a health problem and potential landlord liability.

After the carpets were returned, the tenants complained that the rugs smelled bad. Hal ignored them. At the end of their year, they moved out. When Hal inspected the property, he found that the dogs had ruined the carpets by urinating on them. He was furious and refused to return the deposit.

The tenants countered that the dogs had not urinated. Instead, Hal was smelling the remains of the sewer backup, about which they had complained. The tenants eventually prevailed, and Hal had to return their deposit.

The moral? Even a big deposit is no guarantee!

12

•••◆•••

Moving the Tenant In

First impressions are everything. Real estate agents know that all too well when showing a home to a prospective buyer. The house itself may be wonderful inside, but if it looks shabby, the lawn is filled with weeds and the shrubs and trees are unkempt, that would-be buyer will probably get turned off well before getting past the front door. And no sale will be made.

The same thing applies in a variety of ways to rentals. You've found the tenant, checked out their qualifications, signed a rental agreement and they're ready to move in. Now it's first-impression time all over again. It's their first contact with you as their landlord. How will you come across? If you do it right, you'll go a long way toward having a successful landlord-tenant relationship. Do it wrong, and you'll be setting yourself up for more trouble than you can imagine.

First Things First

As noted in earlier chapters, before the tenant moves in you need to get the money for both the first (and last) month's rent plus all deposits. This money will preferably be in cash or some form of cash equivalent, such as a cashier's check. Practically speaking, however, most tenants will hand over a personal check. If you accept a personal check, take it over to *their* bank (at least this first time) and get it certified. This means that their bank certifies that the funds are available and puts a hold on them—i.e., it pretty much guarantees the funds. This may take you a few minutes, but it's well worth the time.

Landlord's Rule #25 _____

Never let the tenant move in until you have the *cash*. After all, what if you take their personal check to their bank and find that they don't have sufficient funds to cover it?

_____

Once you're satisfied that the money is in hand, you're ready to help the tenants move in.

◆ **CAUTION**   Sometimes after you and the tenants agree upon a move-in date, the tenants will want to move a few of their belongings into the property ahead of time. Although this sounds perfectly innocent, there can be all sorts of problems associated with it.

Keep in mind that as soon as the tenants move anything in, you have, for practical purposes, given them possession. If for any reason you don't go through with renting to them (e.g., they don't come up with all the money, there is a problem with the walk-through or they decide to back out), you have the matter of getting their possessions out of the property. In the old days (again, a long time ago) you might have just taken their stuff and dumped it outside. Not anymore. Now you might actually have to evict them to get it out!

I'm very firm when it comes to moving anything in early. The answer is no. In most cases the tenants can find a friend or relative where things can be stored. At the worst, they can use a public storage facility.

Meeting the New Tenants at the Property

There has to be a time when you officially turn the property over to the tenants. This is usually set up as a combination event. You'll give them the keys, conduct the walk-through (described in detail in Chapter 13), go over any special concerns and hand them an instruction sheet explaining when and where to pay the rent, how to handle moving out and so on. (This sheet is described in detail in Chapter 14.)

This is a very important meeting because it sets the tone for the tenancy. Plan on setting aside an hour or more for the meeting, for you have many things to accomplish.

Locks and Keys

After you've finished the walk-through and you've both signed off on the inspection sheets (as noted, these are described in detail in Chapter 13), you need to give the tenants the keys to the property. It's a good idea to get a receipt for the keys, and it is also possible to incorporate the receipt right into the walk-through sheet. You can include a statement on the sheet saying that the tenants have received a given number of keys. Then have the tenants sign (initial) it.

A word of caution should be given regarding door locks. As the landlord, it is your responsibility to see that you are providing a property that can be properly secured. That means you must have a reasonably safe door lock. Most such locks that you buy in stores will fit this need. (*Note:* For added safety, you may also want to include a throw-bolt, particularly in rental units located in high-crime areas.)

One problem, however, arises if you have a good lock system but then hand over the keys to a new tenant without changing the locks. Unbeknownst to you, the previous tenant could have made an additional key and retained it. He or she could now use the key to easily get back into the property during the occupancy by the new tenants.

Since it costs a fair amount of money to put new locks into a property, one solution is to remove all of the locks and take them to a locksmith. For a relatively small amount of money, the locksmith can rekey them and make sure one key fits both front and back doors. This only works, however, if you have good-quality locks to begin with. Cheap locks often can't be easily rekeyed.

◆

Too Many People with the Same Key

This story is so bizarre that it's almost unbelievable. But I swear it is true.

When I first started in real estate (too long ago to think about), I had a property manager friend whose job was to oversee a large apartment development with hundreds of units. She received rents, took in deposits and in the course of business, handed out keys to tenants. The owner had provided her with an elaborate set of keys, several for each unit, and she took great pains to be sure that each renter received the correct key.

One day when I had brought in a couple who wanted to rent a unit, a tenant came in to complain that his neighbor had gotten into his apartment and, he said, stolen some items. Naturally my property manager friend was quite upset and went to investigate. I went along, too.

It turned out that the owner had not bothered to have each lock separately keyed. Instead, there was only one master key, which opened all of the units. My friend had unknowingly handed out the master to each tenant! There had been no problem until one unscrupulous tenant discovered the fact and took advantage of it.

My friend immediately accosted the owner and demanded an explanation. The owner laughed and said it had worked fine until someone discovered what he had done. "As long as nobody knows," he said, "what's the difference?"

Needless to say, all the locks were rekeyed, and the owner had to make good on the items taken. But that such a thing could happen is almost unbelievable. The moral, of course, is don't let your tenants find out the hard way that you haven't rekeyed the locks. Rekey them automatically every time you get a new tenant. (In some locales rekeying is now a mandatory requirement of the law.)

"Don't Copy" Notice

Furthermore, you can help ensure that tenants don't make extra keys by having the locksmith stamp "do not copy" onto the keys. Surprisingly, it's hard to get any commercial business to make a copy of a key that has those words stamped on it, and it will discourage tenants from making extra keys that are not returned to you on move-out (i.e., keys that could be used to get into the property after the tenant moves out but before you have the locks rekeyed).

Inform Your Tenant about the Rekeying

When I hand over the keys, I always make it a point to note that the locks have all been rekeyed. I then hand the tenants a copy of my receipt from the locksmith showing that the work was done. The tenants frequently say that it's okay, they don't need the receipt, but I insist they look at it. The receipt establishes my credibility and demonstrates my concern for their security.

Items To Give New Tenants

When new tenants move in, I always present them with a number of items that will prove useful to them and will save me a lot of headaches down the road. In one of the bathrooms, usually under the sink, I indicate that I've given them a plumber's helper. This is a plunger that can be used to unplug a toilet. I then proceed to show them how to use it.

A plumber's helper is almost a necessity in any home because toilets get plugged up for a variety of reasons. To use a plunger, you just fill the toilet with water and plunge away, being careful not to slosh water out of the bowl. A tenant who has and uses a plumber's helper can save you the cost of a trip to the property by a plumber. (I also point out that the cost of unplugging clogged plumbing will be born by me if the problem is damaged pipes or roots in the drain system but by the tenants if it's caused by something dropped down the drain, such as toys, sanitary napkins, hairbrushes or whatever.)

I also provide the tenants with an Allen wrench that fits the garbage disposer, assuming the rental unit has one. The Allen wrench goes underneath and allows you to manually turn the garbage disposer, thus clearing it when clogged. I show the tenant how to put the wrench in and turn. A tenant who is good with an Allen wrench can save me lots of trips to the property.

Don't worry about the cost of the plumber's helper and the Allen wrench. Together they are far less than five dollars and well worth the expense.

Show the Tenants How To Use the Appliances

I also carefully explain how to use the various appliances. If the stove has a timer oven (many do), I explain how to use it. I show new tenants how to work the dishwasher and if the unit has a refrigerator, how to set the temperature. Don't assume that tenants automatically know how to work all the appliances. Even if they know how to operate one brand of dishwasher, for example, they may not know how to work the brand in your unit.

If the rental unit has lawn sprinklers that are electrically controlled, I show them where the box is and explain that the sprinklers are set to water on certain days and hours. I ask them what hours they prefer to have the sprinklers come on and then set them. I then ask the tenants not to change the watering settings without calling me first. There are two reasons for this: (1) it's often difficult to set the timers for electric sprinklers, and the tenants might inadvertently set them too often, too seldom or at the wrong times; and (2) if the tenants are paying for the water, there's a tendency for them to set the timers back so the lawns don't get enough water. (See Chapters 5 and 8 for more information.)

◆————————————————————————————

Sally's Neglect To Explain Use of Appliances Results in Headache

Sally rented a 15-year-old home to a couple without explaining the use of the appliances. Later that year during Thanksgiving, she got an emergency call from them saying that the electric oven was broken. They had their Thanksgiving turkey inside, and there was no heat.

Sally sympathized with them and let them cook their bird in her own oven. The next day she sent an electrician out to fix the problem. The electrician reported back, however, that there was no problem. The tenants had inadvertently set the timer on the oven. With the timer activated, the oven wouldn't go on until the designated hour, which happened to be at 2:00 in the morning. The only correction needed was to turn the timer off. He showed the tenants how to do that, and they were mortified but pleased. He also sent Sally a bill for $85.

This true story was one of those situations where Sally was at fault. She hadn't shown the tenants how to use the equipment. If she had, she would have saved herself a lot of trouble and money.

Show the Tenants the Turnoffs

It's also a good idea to walk around the property and show the tenants how to turn off the water, gas and electricity. This is particularly important if your property is subject to flooding where the electrical system can get wet or if it is on the West Coast in earthquake country. After a severe earthquake, you might save your property from being burned down if you quickly turn off the gas.

In addition, I show the tenants exactly where the smoke alarms are located and test each one to show it's working. I also point out the location of the fire extinguisher(s) and any other special feature the unit may have, such as sprinklers or a security alarm system.

Explain about the Utilities

It's a good idea to show the tenants where the garbage is kept if it's an apartment building and explain about not overfilling any dumpsters. If it's a single-family unit, explain what day the garbage is collected and where to place the cans. Also indicate how many cans are allowed and if recyclables are to be separated.

I also provide a list I've drawn up that gives the phone numbers of all the utility companies. That makes it a lot easier for the tenants to have the utilities turned on. The list also provides some other service information. Most of the latter is readily available in the phone book, but presenting it to the tenant on a sheet they can keep handy is useful to them and makes a good impression.

Wishing the New Tenants Well

Finally, I wish the new tenants well and leave. But that's not the end of it.

Over the next few days the tenants will usually be working hard to move in. I try to stop back to see how they're doing and bring them a basket of fruit as a housewarming present. No, it's hardly necessary. But I once read that when you do more than people expect, you get results beyond what you anticipate. This is the extra bit that makes the difference.

A good landlord will continue keeping a business relationship with tenants. This doesn't mean going overboard as did Sally with the tenant who wanted to become her best friend. Rather, send a card at Christmas or Hanukkah, and know which is appropriate for your tenant. Call or stop by every month or two to see how things are going, and ask if there's anything you can do to make the place better. (Most landlords never come by as long as the tenant doesn't call to complain. That's usually a mistake on two counts. First, the only time a tenant sees such a landlord is when he or she is complaining, and that sours the relationship. Second, by stopping by early, you can often catch problems in the bud and avoid bigger costs down the road.)

Help your tenants move in. Make things as easy as possible for them. They might do the same for you later on.

13

◆◆◆◆◆◆◆

The Move-in Walk-Through Inspection

No area of landlord-tenant relations is more contentious with more complaints and lawsuits than that of the return of the deposit. I have yet to find a landlord who doesn't feel that he or she is entitled to at least a portion of the cleaning deposit when the tenant leaves. Similarly, tenants automatically seem to assume that they are entitled to the return of all of the cleaning deposit.

Quite frankly, the truth lies somewhere in between. From my position I see the reasoning of landlords quite clearly. On the other hand, I've been a tenant once or twice, just enough to know how it feels not to get a cleaning deposit back when I felt I was entitled to one.

◆

The Tenant's Perspective on Cleaning Deposits

Many years ago when I was right out of college, my wife and I rented a small house. We had a dog, which was okay with the landlord, and a $100 cleaning deposit, which in those days was a lot of money for us. We kept the house clean and when we moved, we did a thorough job of cleaning. We shampooed the carpets, waxed the floors and cleaned everything. Then we asked for our cleaning deposit back.

To this day (decades later) I remember the landlord walking through the house saying, "Yes, you've done a remarkable job of cleaning up the property. But you had a dog in here, so there's bound to be hidden damage, particularly to the carpeting. I'm keeping all of the deposit." And that was it. He kept it all. There was really nothing to be done back then.

I like to tell this story to landlords because when you own and manage property, you see so much of the other side of things. These days I'm used to tenants who leave carpets torn and stained, walls marked, stoves filthy with grease, toilets and sinks lined with filth . . . well, presumably you're a landlord, and I don't have to say more. You've seen it, too. The tenants who leave the biggest mess are frequently the same ones who holler the loudest when demanding their cleaning deposits back.

It's easy enough to get permanently inured to tenants' requests for the return of cleaning deposits. However, just keep in mind that there are good tenants out there, and even those who don't leave the property up to your standards may indeed have spent considerable time and effort trying to get the place back into shape. From their perspective, they are entitled to a sizable chunk, if not all, of the deposit back.

Can You Keep the Cleaning Deposit?

The basic rules have not changed much, although the actual practice has shifted enormously. As landlords know, the rule is that tenants must leave the property in about the same condition as they found it, *normal wear and tear excepted*. It's this last part, however, that often trips up landlords.

What Can Happen When the Landlord Fails To Use the Proper Paint

Hal rented out a two-bedroom, two-bath apartment to a couple who had children. When the couple moved out, he discovered that there were marks from colored pencils, crayons and other materials on the bathroom walls. He had hired a cleaning crew to wash down the bathroom walls; however, it turned out that when Hal had painted the apartment a year earlier, he hadn't used high-gloss paint in the bathrooms. Instead, he had used standard flat wall paint. As a consequence, when a cleaning person tried washing the paint, she only smeared the marks. The paint couldn't be washed. So Hal called in a painter to repaint both bathrooms. Then he charged the cost of both the failed cleaning and the repainting to the tenant by withholding the amount, now up to around $300, from the cleaning deposit.

The tenant protested and eventually took Hal to small-claims court. There the tenant agreed that Hal was indeed entitled to the cost of cleaning the bathrooms—about $100. However, he was not entitled to the cost of repainting, about $200, since he hadn't originally painted the baths with the right kind of paint normally used for bathrooms—the kind that could be washed. The judge agreed, and Hal had to return $200 of the deposit to the tenants.

This story illustrates two points. The first is that you have to be very careful about how to characterize money you withhold from the cleaning deposit. If the tenant can say the damage is caused by normal wear and tear, or in Hal's case by the landlord's own actions, he or she may be entitled to all or a portion of the deposit back. There's a gray area, however, when determining what constitutes damage and what is normal wear and tear.

Second, if you aren't careful, the tenants can take you to court, sue you over the cleaning deposit and possibly win. In Hal's case the tenant only got a portion of the cleaning deposit back. However, if you violate state laws regarding the return of a cleaning deposit, you could also be liable for fines.

Rules for Returning Cleaning Deposits

Most states today require the landlord to do two things with regard to a cleaning deposit:

- If you don't return the entire deposit, you must give the tenant a complete accounting of where the money was spent.

- You must return the deposit or a portion of it along with the accounting within a maximum period of time, often as short a time as 14 days.

Just following the guidelines, of course, doesn't mean that you're home free. If the tenants disagree with your accounting, particularly the amount you have withheld, they can take you to court, usually small-claims court, and sue to recover all or part of their cleaning deposit. Since many courts these days tend to look with favor on tenants' complaints in these matters, it's now up to you to substantiate your claims for damage.

◆───────────────────────────────────────

Landlord's Hint

If the tenant leaves the place a mess and you hire someone to clean it up, generally speaking you can deduct the cost of the cleanup from the cleaning deposit. On the other hand, if you clean up the place yourself, while you can deduct your cost of materials, you probably cannot deduct a figure for your time spent.

───────────────────────────────────────

Documenting the Condition of the Property

We'll have much more to say about deposits and how you handle your costs when the tenant leaves the property in a mess in Chapter 14, which details the move-out walk-through inspection. But for now let's consider just what you can do to protect yourself when the tenant moves in.

Probably the best—and perhaps the only—thing you can do to avoid big arguments and possible lawsuits when a tenant moves out, is to document *before* and *after*. You must show how the property looked before the tenant moved in and then how it looked after the tenant moved out.

While it is true that arguments can grow over the cost of certain repairs, the most common area of disagreement is over what the property looked like before move-in. The landlord usually says that the unit was in perfect shape, while the tenant claims it was a mess from the beginning. Who's right? Keep in mind that today many courts tend to favor tenants' claims over those of landlords.

Film and Video Documentation

Some landlords who have been burned by tenants who argued successfully that the rental unit was in bad shape when they moved in have taken to recording the initial condition of the property through the use of a camera and/or a camcorder. The idea is that before renting, you walk through the property and visually prepare a record of the condition of floors, walls, appliances and so on. Thus, when the tenant moves out and claims that the property was not clean or newly painted or whatever, you have a visual record to prove otherwise.

Nevertheless, there are certain problems inherent in a visual record. First, there's the cost. To document every room on film requires many rolls as well as careful photography, including a special close-up lens. Second, as those who are sophisticated in the field know, you can make any wall, for example, look clean or full of scratches just by how you illuminate it. Thus, you need to have good, neutral lighting and expensive equipment. In short, unless your hobby is photography, taking pictures before move-in can be more hassle than it's worth. Furthermore, since you don't know where damage might occur, you must photograph everything in detail to be sure you have a clean "before" picture—a daunting task. (This is not to say that taking pictures of *damage* is not worthwhile. Pictures clearly showing damage can help your case immensely, as we'll see in Chapter 14.)

Camcorders do a better job, simply because they are more realistic. You can easily pan across a floor and wall and in a few moments capture almost everything. The trouble with camcorders, however, comes with playback. You need a playback VCR (the camcorder itself will do) and a TV set. Setting all this up can be a hassle. Then you must search through the original tape for just the right "before" shot. All of this can be very impractical.

Finally, with any kind of visual records the tenant can dispute *when* you shot the original, saying the condition wasn't that way when he or she moved in. One landlord I know attempts to solve this problem by having an independent person, such as a neighbor, walk through while he's videotaping and say the date and time. (To prove when the film or tape was taken, I've heard that you can tape or photograph the tenants themselves, getting them right in the picture. I find that impossible, however, as a practical matter. You certainly can't get the tenants in every shot, and it may be more than a little demeaning to have them walk around, backing up to walls, carpets, etc. No good tenant will put up with that for a minute.)

In short, visual records can be helpful, but in my experience their aid is more in the area of secondary support to back up what you've otherwise demonstrated to be the case, particularly with damage after the move-out.

If a visual record doesn't work, how do you demonstrate the condition of the rental before the tenants move in? What's worked for me and a lot of property managers over the years is a proper move-in walk-through inspection sheet. This goes a long way toward substantiating the true condition of the rental.

Walk-Through Inspection Sheets

I have a friend, a property manager for more than 20 years, who swears by the walk-through sheets shown in Appendix B. She says that she has been called to court by tenants on a number of occasions and has always won as a result of those sheets.

What's so impressive about walk-through sheets? It's the fact that they are written documentation *signed by both you, the landlord, and the tenants.* It's very hard for a tenant to later say that a wall was marked or a stove was filthy when he or she has signed that both were clean and in good condition at move-in.

After you've approved the tenants and received the rent but before handing over the keys and as a condition of renting, they must go with you through the property with the sheets. The tenants are made aware that the purpose of the move-in walk-through inspection sheet is to document the condition of the property before taking possession, and it's to their advantage to note any problems. You'll almost never find a tenant who isn't willing or eager to go through this process.

Room by Room

Note that the walk-through sheets are for each room. There is one for each bedroom, bathroom, dining room, living room, hallway, kitchen and other area. No area of the house should be left out, including closets.

Furthermore, the sheets note the condition of the walls, ceilings, floors, windows, screens, fixtures, appliances—in short, everything in the house. And they specifically state that each item is *without damage and clean, having no marks except as noted.* There is a place where any dirt, marks, scratches or damage should be noted. My property manager friend insists that her tenants not only sign at the end of the list but initial each sheet as well and initial important items such as the stove (a big area of contention over cleanliness), the sink, the refrigerator and so on.

Conducting the Walk-Through

There's a psychology involved in the move-in walk-through. Remember, it's done *before* the tenants move anything into the property—before they take possession. As a result, there isn't any pressure (as there is at move-out) for the tenants to worry that the landlord will say they did anything. Rather, they are looking for faults, and you, as the landlord, often have to defend the condition of the property! (It's another reason to be sure that each time you rent a property, it's in tip-top shape.)

Furthermore, there's usually an upbeat feeling of good cheer during the walk-through. After all, the tenants have nothing to worry about— they haven't moved in yet and can't be blamed for anything wrong. Since the tenancy is just starting, they naturally want to be on a good footing with you. Hence, at this time they are least likely to exaggerate a problem. After all, if they insist that there's a big hole in the carpet and there's no hole there, you won't be very likely to give them the key to move in.

On the other hand, most tenants will be scrupulously careful going over these sheets with you. They will carefully point out every mark, scratch, tear and other dirty or damaged part of the rental unit. After all, they understand well that anything that does not go on this sheet will come back to haunt them when they move out.

Getting an Accurate Description

Therefore, it is absolutely necessary that you come up with very *precise* language to describe any exceptions to "clean and undamaged" that you write down. For example, there may be a mark in a wall caused when the previous tenant hit it with a dresser while moving out. If you write down "back wall of bedroom is marked," you could be in for real trouble. When the new tenant moves out, that wall could be covered from floor to ceiling with marks; but when you protest, the tenant will point to the walk-through, saying, "See, you wrote down that the wall was marked!"

My property manager friend always writes down something specific such as, "Small single mark on back wall approximately two inches long by half an inch wide." That pretty much limits any claim that the whole wall was marked.

Don't Forget Safety Features

Almost every area of the country today requires rentals to be equipped with smoke detectors. The move-in walk-through is an excellent time to note not only that your rental unit has a smoke detector but that it is in working condition. Have tenants sign (or initial) the sheet to say that they've seen the smoke detector and have tested it themselves.

Some locations also require fire extinguishers. Be sure the tenants sign that they have noted the location of the extinguisher and that it is full and in working condition.

Working with the Tenant

There are, of course, bound to be areas of dispute. One of the most common is the carpeting. A tenant may say that the carpeting looks old and worn. You may say that it's nearly new and fresh. How do you come up with a description that you can both live with?

One answer that my property manager friend has is to list the age of the carpet (as evidenced by her bill of sale) and the last time it was cleaned (as evidenced by her invoice from the carpet-cleaning company). It's hard for a tenant to argue with these two items. Any specific damage or wear, such as cigarette burns or stains, can be noted as to size and location.

PART THREE

◆◆◆◆◆◆◆

Moving Tenants Out

14

◆◆◆◆◆◆◆

Achieving a Friendly Move-out

You should never think of tenants as permanent. All tenants leave sooner or later. Therefore, the goal of a good landlord is to make that eventual move-out as painless and as cost-free (to you) as possible. That means taking active steps to ensure that things go smoothly.

Landlord's Rule #26

You always have to pay close attention to your properties, especially when tenants are moving in, are moving out and are in-between.

Advance Preparations

Good property managers know that the time to get started preparing for when the tenant moves out is on the day the tenant moves in. On move-in day many good managers will hand their new tenants a printed sheet explaining just what's expected of them, including the procedure for moving out. It includes such things as giving notice and leaving the place clean. Don't think that all tenants automatically know how they are supposed to conduct themselves when they move out. Many are completely in the dark unless you tell them.

Figure 14.1 is a moving instructions sheet that covers a number of areas important to the tenant and vital to you. Let's consider each area in turn.

Giving Proper Notice

Assuming that you're renting on a month-to-month basis, you will expect 30 days' notice (or whatever you've agreed upon) before the tenant moves out. But just what constitutes notice? I once had a tenant who included a note with a rent payment, saying, "We will be moving soon." A month later, they came by to drop off the key. When I asked what was up, they said they had given me written notice of their intention to move.

Inform the tenant that you expect them to let you know the *exact date* when they intend to move out. For practical purposes, in most cases this will be in the form of a phone call. However, ideally they should send you a written note. And presumably their notice will be at least 30 days (or whatever you've agreed upon) before they move.

You should also indicate that the notice must be given within 30 days of the next rent payment, so that the tenants understand that they will need to move on the 1st (presumably when the rent is due), not sometime in the middle of the following month.

A good idea is to include a tear-off at the bottom of the sheet that the tenants can send back to you, specifying just when they will move out.

◆
_____

Landlord's Hint

If the tenant must move sometime other than on the rental date, you can, of course, agree to another date. However, I would insist on the rent being paid until the 1st. If it's a tenant who's given you trouble, you may be happy to see him or her go and may be willing to compromise by splitting the difference.

_____

FIGURE 14.1   Moving Instructions Sheet

Dear Tenant:

At some point you will be moving from the premises you now occupy. In order to help make that move easier and to avoid confusion, I have prepared the following instructions. They will let you know what's expected of you on move-out according to the terms of your rental agreement.

What Is Proper Notice?

If you have a month-to-month tenancy, you are required by the terms of your rental agreement to give a minimum of ___ days' notice before moving. That notice:

1. should be in writing (see the tear-out at the bottom);

2. should give the exact *date* you intend to move; and

3. the move-out date should be 30 days from your last rent payment. For example, if you pay on the 1st, you should plan to move on the 1st of the following month.

If your plans change and you cannot move out on the day you have designated, please let me know as soon as possible and I will try to make arrangements for you to stay longer. Be aware, however, that in many cases new tenants will be waiting to move in. Also, you will be charged for any additional days you stay.

What Returning Possession Means

You will not be considered to have moved out and returned possession of the premises until *all* of your personal property (every bit of furniture, clothing, utensils, towels, boxes and so on) has been removed from the premises, including the garage, walkways, utility room and any other areas you occupy, and you have returned *all* sets of keys. Rent will not stop until all of your property has been removed (assuming also that you have given proper notice).

Please call me at _____ at least three days in advance to make arrangements to return keys and to have a move-out inspection.

What Is Required To Get Your Security Deposit Back?

To get a complete refund of your security deposit, you must leave the premises clean and without damage, normal wear and tear excepted, return keys and

---

FIGURE 14.1 Moving Instructions Sheet (Continued)

---

fulfill all the obligations of your rental agreement. If you have damaged the premises or left it unclean, a portion of your deposit may be used to pay for repairs, to clean areas that were left dirty (pay special attention to stoves, toilets, tubs, sinks, sills and floors) and to pay for pet or other damage. Any unused portion of your security deposit will be returned within ___ days along with a complete written accounting of money spent.

If there are marks on walls, please call me before attempting to clean them, or else you could make them worse. Before shampooing carpets or cleaning wall coverings, please call me so that I can let you know which types of cleaning will work on the materials you have and will not cause damage.

Your Responsibilities
It is your responsibility to call all utility companies to have service discontinued and to turn off phone, trash and newspaper service. It is your responsibility to leave the premises in a clean and undamaged condition.

Tear off at the dotted line and mail to landlord when you plan to move out.
- -
Tenant's Name:

Address: _____

Day of month rent is paid:_____

To:
Landlord's name: _____

Landlord's address: _____

You are hereby given notice that as per our rental agreement, we are giving you ____ days' notice (___ days' minimum notice is required) of our intention to move. We understand that we are responsible to pay rent until the end of the notice period.

Date of move-out: _____

Signed by tenant:_____

Let the Tenant Know What *Moving Out* Means

Moving out means that they will have *all* of their possessions out of the house and the garage. Everything will be gone. There won't be clothes left hanging in a closet, boxes in the bedroom or cooking utensils in the kitchen. *Everything out* means just that. Emphasize that you can't consider them out until they are fully out and have turned possession of everything in the rental back to you. Letting your tenants know that you will require them to pay rent until everything is out usually guarantees compliance.

How and When the Deposits Will Be Returned

Having a procedure and letting the tenants know what it is up front avoids confusion and unhappiness at the end. Let the tenants know you expect the property to be left in the same condition it was found, excepting normal wear and tear, and explain exactly what you mean.

Let them know that you will deduct from their deposits the costs for repairing any damage. If you have a pet deposit, indicate that you'll deduct from this any damage the pet may do. Indicate that any repair work will be done at the current market rate by professionals in the field, not by you. (If you do repair work yourself, many tenants will assume your time is free and won't expect to be charged for it. Indeed, it may be illegal for you to charge for *your time* spent on repair work on your own property in your state or area.)

Also let them know that they will receive the money back within 14 days (or as specified by the laws in your state) along with a complete accounting. This is a good place to put a notice in big type that the cleaning/security deposit may not be used as the last month's rent.

How the Keys Are To Be Returned

At some point the tenants return possession of the property to you. This is normally done after they have removed all of their personal property and is evidenced by the return of the keys to you.

Be sure you let them know that you want *all* the keys returned. Even though you change the locks, you don't want someone out there who even thinks he or she can still get back in.

Explain about the Utilities and Phone

Normally the landlord has the utilities turned on for cleanup and showing on the same date as the tenant moves out. Point out that if they move later than the appointed date, they'll also be charged a prorated cost for utilities they use.

When They Let You Know They're Going To Move

As soon as you get wind of the fact that your tenants are going to move, it's a good idea to send them another one of the moving instructions sheets. They may have lost the original, and this acts as a good reminder.

Letter of Recommendation

If the tenant who is moving was a good tenant who always paid on time and didn't cause problems, I usually call and ask them if they would like a letter of recommendation for their next landlord. Most tenants are astounded at this offer and, of course, happily accept.

I have no problem recommending a good tenant to someone else. Furthermore, giving the tenant this letter often puts them in such a friendly state of mind that they do an extra good job of cleaning up the property, just to live up to what I've said about them! (See Figure 14.2 for a sample letter of recommendation.)

Note that if your tenants move out in order to purchase a property, their new mortgage lender will almost certainly request a formal letter (sent to you by the mortgage company) asking for specifics on the tenant. If you give a copy to the tenant to show how you recommended him or her, it will serve the same purpose as a separate letter of recommendation.

Confirm Dates

A good landlord quickly learns not to leave anything to guesswork or chance. If your tenants, for example, say they will be out by August 1st, call them in the middle of July to confirm the date. Also confirm that

---

FIGURE 14.2 Tenant's Letter of Recommendation

Date:_____

To Whom It May Concern:

This will recommend *(tenant's name)* to you. *(Tenant's name)* has been my tenant from _____ to _____. During that time the rent was always paid promptly, there was no damage done to the premises, the yard was well kept and there were no unusual problems. When the tenant moved out, the property was left in a clean and undamaged condition.

I consider *(tenant's name)* to be an excellent tenant.

Sincerely,

_____
(Landlord)

---

they received the move-out instructions sheet. And reconfirm that they understand what's required to get the cleaning/security deposit back.

No, it shouldn't be necessary for you to go this extra step. But if you don't, there will come a time when you think they're moving out on one day and they'll be moving out on another. Think of it as being paranoid. Think of it as another case of whatever can go wrong, will. Think of it anyway you like. Only reconfirm by phone.

When it gets closer to the actual move-out date—say, a few days before—call again. Arrange for a time for the tenants to meet you in the rental to go through the move-out walk-through. Also emphasize that at that time, they will need to return the keys and have all of their personal property out of the house.

◆ Landlords Must Pay Attention to Move-out Dates

Hal had a rental on the other side of town. It was a good property that rented easily, but he had to take the busy crosstown expressway to get to it, and that was inconvenient, so he went out there as rarely as possible.

One day his tenants called to let him know they'd be moving the next month, and he made a mental note of it. They called again a week before they were to move and let him know it would be on Sunday and they'd be out by noon. He could come by at that time, check out the property and get the keys back. Hal again made a mental note of the conversation, which he promptly forgot.

It was a week and a half later on a Wednesday that Hal thought about the rental, mainly because he hadn't received the rent. He then remembered that the tenants said they were moving on the previous Sunday. He called them but learned the phone was disconnected, so he drove out to the rental, much to his irritation, on the busy crosstown freeway.

He found the front door open and the tenants gone. The flooring and carpeting was a mess because neighborhood kids had apparently wandered in with muddy shoes and tracked their feet on it. Other than that, however, it was clean and in good shape. The keys were on the counter, along with a note saying the tenants had cleaned the apartment and waited for him that Sunday until 2:00 P.M.. They had called but were unable to get through. When they had to leave, they locked the doors and left the keys on the counter as well as a forwarding address for the return of their deposit.

Hal promptly had the apartment cleaned and deducted the cost along with the three days that elapsed until he picked up the keys. The tenants protested. They said they had made every effort to contact Hal and return the keys on the day they left. They said they had left the apartment spotless and the doors locked and had no idea how the neighborhood kids got in. And they produced a copy of their letter to Hal that they had left on the counter.

Hal wanted to stonewall them but on advice from a property manager friend, decided to avoid a hassle when he was told he couldn't win. He returned all of their deposit. After all, the loss of three days and the extra cleaning were entirely due to his own lack of attention.

Meeting with the Tenants at Move-out Time

When you meet with your tenants on the appointed day for their departure, immediately check to see that they are completely out of the rental unit. Furniture, boxes, clothing and so forth left anywhere indicates that they are not completely out. You should point this out to them and indicate that you can't proceed until they have *all* of their possessions removed. If necessary, tell them you'll come by later, although you can emphasize that this will be an inconvenience to you. If it takes them another day to get their goods out, point out that it will cost them a day's worth of rent.

Assuming that they are completely out, ask them for the keys to the unit, making sure they return all sets. Once they have moved their personal property out and have given you the keys, they have returned possession to you.

Now it's time to go over the move-out walk-through inspection sheet with them. (You can do this before you receive the keys, of course, but I like to get the keys first, as this indicates that they are finished with the cleaning.)

The Move-out Walk-Through Inspection

The inspection sheet is the exact same one you used for the tenants when they moved in. You've presumably kept it safely stored, awaiting the day they moved out.

Produce the sheet, or a Xerox copy of the sheet, and then go over it, room by room, with the tenants. Along the way you discover any damage that's more than normal wear and tear, and you and the tenants account for it, indicating what damage will be deducted from their cleaning deposit.

When you're finished and you've agreed upon damages—if not exact amounts—everyone shakes hands and the tenancy is successfully concluded.

Not likely. That's the ideal scenario, but in actual practice it's rarely that simple. Let's consider what is more likely to happen.

The Tenants Don't Show Up for the Move-out Walk-Through Inspection

But it's to their advantage to show up! They can be right on hand to dispute any damage that you feel may have been done. They can point to the inspection record and note that the damage was right there before they moved in.

True. In most cases tenants will show up for the move-out walk-through inspection. But in many cases they won't. Maybe their schedule makes it impossible for them to be there. Maybe they left the place in such a mess that they're too embarrassed to show up. Or maybe they just can't handle the apparent confrontation involved in walking through the property with you.

In any event, it isn't necessary for the tenants to be there for the move-out walk-through inspection. Their not being present doesn't prevent you from conducting the inspection yourself; it only weakens their position should they dispute anything you say later on.

My own feeling is that if the tenants aren't there for the move-out walk-through inspection, I want to document anything I find. This can mean having a neutral third party, such as a neighbor, walk through with me and indicate in writing that what we found is indeed the way it was. Or it could also include taking photos or videos of damage. (Remember, in Chapter 13 I noted the problem taking photos or videos beforehand because it is difficult to photograph clean areas since you can't predict where the damage will occur. Now there's no problem. You can zero right in on the damage.)

The Tenants Show Up and Walk Through with You But Deny They Did Any of the Damage

This is what can happen. You walk into a bedroom, and there are crayon marks all over the walls. You point this out to the tenant and say that this can't be washed off without ruining the paint. Instead the walls will have to be thoroughly washed and then painted twice, once with a sealer to keep any remaining crayon marks from bleeding through and a second time for the actual painting.

The tenants look aghast and say that their kids couldn't possibly have done the damage. Perhaps they did a little bit of it, but the walls were definitely marked beforehand. Now you both turn to the sheet on this bedroom that the tenants initialed when they first moved in and look to see what's written there. You hope it will say, "All walls clean and freshly painted—no marks or scratches of any kind." Then what can the tenants argue about?

Instead, however, the sheet says, "Walls generally clean with a few marks and scratches." "Aha!" the tenants say, "See, we told you. It was marked up before we moved in."

Once again this points out the importance of being extremely careful and precise when you fill out the walk-through sheets. Remember to list each mark by size, shape and location.

You will be hard-pressed to keep any of the tenant's cleaning/security deposit if your own sheets note that there were marks and scratches on the walls before they moved in. On the other hand, you'll be in an excellent position to use the deposit to clean up the damage if your sheets indicate that no marks or scratches were there beforehand.

Landlord's Rule #27

Always paint and clean your rental thoroughly before the tenants move in. That way you'll be able to write down a clean bill of health on the move-in walk-through inspection sheet, which will provide you with the evidence you need to collect for damages when you conduct the move-out walk-through inspection.

The Tenants Agree They Did the Damage But Now Want To Correct It Themselves

If you did your move-in walk-through sheet correctly, there really won't be much disputing who did the damage to your rental. There will be the tenants' own signatures and initials on a written document, saying there were no marks, scratches and so on when they moved in. And now here's the damage. Yes, they can still always deny it, but anyone based in reality will see that theirs is a losing cause.

So now a tenant may say, "Yes, I didn't realize how marked up those walls really were. I'm surprised, but I'd like the opportunity to correct it myself."

Landlord's Rule #28

Allowing the tenant who did the damage to correct it after they move out is like giving an award to the person who helps put out the fire in your barn, after they first set it.

This is a trap that is very difficult to avoid. The tenants have already moved out and, presumably, given you the keys. Now they want the opportunity to go back and clean up or fix damage that you both agree they did.

You may argue that they should have corrected the damage before they moved. However, if the tenant now gets angry and eventually sues you, they can argue that they offered to fix the damage once it was revealed to them, but you didn't give them the opportunity to do so. Not giving them the opportunity to correct a problem, once it's revealed, could mean you lose.

You may be in a lose-lose situation. If you don't give the tenant the opportunity to fix or clean up the property, it could come back to haunt you. But if you do give them the opportunity, it could be even worse.

When the Tenant "Corrects" the Problem

In our previous example there were crayon marks on the walls. The problem is that the grease in crayons bleeds through most paints. The easiest way to handle this is to wash, seal and repaint.

However, a tenant who has already vacated the premises isn't likely to want to take the time to go through the various steps, which can take a few days. When this situation once happened to me and I let the tenant attempt the cleanup, she used a heavy industrial cleaner on the walls, rubbing hard to remove the crayon marks. Not the easiest way to go but very thorough. Too thorough.

She did remove the marks, but she also removed the paint and some of the plaster where she had rubbed. Now instead of crayon marks, there were paintless areas and gouges in the plaster that stood out distinctly from the other areas of the wall. It would require not only painting but replastering and retexturing to correct. The price was going up. The tenant, however, proudly pointed to the area upon reinspection and dared me to find any crayon marks on the wall!

In a situation where a tenant wants time to correct a problem, I try to point out the obvious. In attempting to correct the problem, it may become worse. Furthermore, I now have possession and must get in quickly to clean up so that the property can be shown and rerented.

When I point out the problems involved and the timing concerns, tenants frequently back off from their desire to correct a problem themselves. I've found that most tenants who do damage aren't really that anxious to spend a lot of physical effort correcting the problem.

Disputes over Price

Matters may now evolve to the question of how much it will cost to have the work done. As I mentioned, I no longer do the work myself. Now we're talking about having someone come in, wash the wall, seal it and then repaint. How much will that cost?

I have a handyman who can do this kind of work for around $50 per wall plus the cost of the materials. I give that figure to the tenants, who, figuring it's worth it, may acquiesce just to avoid any hassle.

This, however, brings up a point that's in dispute among property managers. Some managers prepare a pricing chart, an actual list of prices for various services they may perform on a rental. There's a price for cleaning a clogged drain and repainting a wall with crayon marks on it. There's a price for fixing a broken window and cleaning a stain out of a carpet. In short, there's a price listed for almost everything.

When there's a dispute, the landlord brings out the list, points to the price for repainting a wall with crayon marks and says, "That's $65, including materials." There it is in black and white. It's so clear-cut and easy. Many managers will even make their pricing list available to tenants when they first move in and again when they give notice that they are moving out so that there won't be any confusion over costs.

Lists are indeed neat and clean, and I have no argument with those who use them. But I don't like them myself for two reasons. First, prices change and change often. That means I would have to be constantly updating my list. I'm simply not well organized enough to be doing that all the time for a whole variety of costs. Besides, I find that much of the work is done by handymen, and they change frequently and tend to charge differently.

Second, lists tend to be overly restrictive. By that I mean that the problem may not fit the list's description or the price given. For example, if the drain is clogged, how much does the list indicate to charge? It all depends, of course, on what the problem is. It could be only $55 to have the rooter man come out and run a snake through the lines. Or it could be $700 to dig up a blockage caused by a steel rod that was flushed down the line until it wedged at an elbow joint. (This happened to me when I rented to a mechanic who worked in a body and fender shop. His child somehow got one of his tools into the drain system.)

After a while you get a pretty good idea of what things will cost, and you can give an *estimate* to the tenant right on the spot. If, on the other hand, the tenant doesn't like your price or you're not sure of the cost, you can say, "I'll have someone come in to look at it immediately, and he'll tell me the cost. I'll get back to you on that." Admittedly, this isn't the best of all possible solutions since it takes time. But it does have the advantage of producing a truly accurate price. And quite frankly, by the next day the tenant is even less inclined to dispute the price.

The Value of Having the Tenant Walk Through with You

As difficult as it can be at times, having the tenant go through the move-out walk-through inspection with you has one enormous benefit. You usually end up with agreement at the end.

The tenant's presence forces you to be fair in your estimates (not that you wouldn't anyhow, of course). Your presence forces the tenant to see things from your perspective and acknowledge that some damage may have actually been done.

In short, the tenant is more likely to accept deductions from the cleaning/security deposit after the walk-through. And in my opinion, he or she is far less likely to feel angry and get into a dispute with you that ends up in court. In other words, even though at times it can be hard on the blood pressure, walking through with a tenant can end up being the most amicable way of ending a tenancy, especially one that will involve deductions from the tenant's deposit.

When To Return the Deposit

As noted earlier, you must give the deposit money back promptly in accordance with the laws of your state. But remember to keep the deposit long enough to uncover any hidden damage that may have occurred.

I have on occasion given back a portion (as much as half) of the deposit right on the spot at the time the tenant moved out when, after going through the move-out walk-through inspection, nothing obvious appeared. Yes, I realize this isn't good property management practice since a large hidden cost can crop up later, but I do sympathize with tenants who worry about somebody else holding their money and who need it right away to move into another property. I also think I have a pretty good feeling for problems that are likely to occur. I haven't been burned yet by doing this, but there's no doubt I could get into trouble in the future. It's just what makes me feel comfortable as a landlord.

You, of course, have to make your own decisions.

15

◆◆◆◆◆◆◆

The Tenant Who Won't Move Out

The worst thing that can happen to you as a landlord is to have a tenant who won't pay rent and won't move. On the other hand, many experienced landlords argue that their worst nightmare is a rental unit that's been trashed. I maintain that if you have a tenant who won't pay and won't move, the trashing of your rental may only be days away anyhow.

Before going further, let's be clear about what this topic isn't. We're not talking about tenants who are late paying or who promise to move on the 15th and then say they can't get out until the 17th. Those problems do occur and when they happen, may seem monumental. But in fact they are trivial when compared to the tenant who locks the doors, won't let you in, won't pay the rent and won't quit the property.

Eviction

The word that landlords universally hate to say is *eviction*. The reason is that it's psychologically traumatic—certainly for the beginning landlord—and costly. Let's focus in on the costs.

When tenants go sour, it usually doesn't happen all at once. It occurs over time. Maybe they're late with the rent one month. The next month they're late again, and you, being the kind-hearted soul you are, give them a few more days. In any event, let's say that a week goes by before you give them the first eviction notice. (We'll discuss eviction proce-dures in Chapter 16.)

They don't respond, and after a few more days you decide that you have no alternative but to start eviction proceedings in earnest. You've already lost a week and a half of rent.

Landlord's Rule #29 _____

If you have a tenant evicted, the chances are almost certain that the property will be left trashed.

_____

Now you go to court to have the tenants removed. These actions normally come first on the court calendar, so you get your day in court quite soon. But the judge sees that you are holding the equivalent of a month's rent in the cleaning/security deposit. In my experience few judges will rule in your favor until the tenants have used up their cleaning/security deposit—that is, until at least a month has passed without their paying the rent. This is doubly so if the tenants show up with a tale of woe. (Note: eviction proceedings go by different names. In some states, they are called *unlawful detainer*; in others, *suit for posses-sion*. Check for your local terminology and procedures.)

So let's say that you ultimately prevail and the tenants are evicted within six weeks. (Six weeks is typical for eviction actions, provided the tenants don't protest or countersue. See Chapter 16.) Now you have your rental unit back. But what has it cost you?

Costs to You of an Eviction

Lost rent—6 weeks	$1,500	(assuming a rental rate of $1,000 per month)
Cleaning and repairing	1,500	(assuming the unit was only moderately trashed)
Legal fees	1,000	
Total	$4,000	

Thus, assuming that things go fairly well, a unit that's renting for $1,000 a month may cost you around $4,000 in an eviction, including lost rent and expenses. That works out to about four months of rent.

Losing the equivalent of four or more months of rent can be devastating to many landlord-owners who are on a razor-thin margin anyway. It's enough to throw a property into a negative cash flow situation, sometimes for years. Besides, we haven't even considered the aggravation.

◆───────────────────────────────────────

Sally's Eviction Experience

Sally rented a home to a family with three kids and three dogs. After four months of paying the rent on time, they called and said both the husband and wife had lost their jobs and couldn't pay their rent, now due. But they were looking for other jobs and would pay as soon as possible.

Sally was sympathetic but said she had to get the rent to make her mortgage payments. Without the rent, she could lose the property. They were sympathetic but said they simply had no money. So she asked them to move. They said they would, when they could.

Sally began eviction proceedings. In the meantime she sent a note to her lender (who had the mortgage on the property), explaining that the rent would be late. A lender's representative called back to say that the lender didn't care about Sally's rental problems; it wanted the money on time, or it would start foreclosure. (Many lenders will threaten but will actually wait months before beginning foreclosure, especially in a weak sales market.)

Sally couldn't sleep at night worrying about her property, so she borrowed money on her credit card to make the mortgage payment. Then she borrowed more to pay her attorney, who was handling the eviction.

Then the tenants began calling and pleaded with Sally to let them stay, saying they had no place to move. Sally felt she was being pressured on all sides—by the tenants, by the lender and even by her attorney, who always seemed to need more money.

Eventually Sally got the tenants out, but not before she had many sleepless nights and a great deal of worrying. The experience was enough to make her want to sell all her properties and forget entirely about rentals.

Add the aggravation to the expense and you quickly realize why landlords hate evictions. They are nothing but trouble for everyone concerned. They also are the reason why most landlords will go to all sorts of extremes to avoid going through the process of court-ordered eviction. Nine out of ten landlords will tell you that they will try almost anything before resorting to eviction.

That's the reason why for the remainder of this chapter we will consider the alternatives to judicial eviction of tenants who won't pay.

Try Reasoning

Talking with your tenant has enormous advantages, if you do it correctly. For one thing, it doesn't cost you any money. For another, it doesn't take much time. And for a third, if you play your cards right, it might result in the tenant moving out quickly without your having to go to court.

Keep in mind that we're not discussing a tenant who's late with the rent. We're talking about a tenant who won't pay and won't move. At some point you've already decided that this tenant is a lost cause, and all you want is to have him or her out. Yes, go ahead and serve the three-day notice; it might just be the incentive needed. Even go ahead and begin unlawful detainer action. But along the way, take time to talk. Here are some things you can talk about.

Tell the Tenants Your Situation

If you've done your homework, you've established rapport with your tenants from the moment they moved in. They may not consider you a bosom buddy, but they probably don't feel a great deal of antagonism toward you either. After all, they realize they've instigated this problem (unless there's a dispute over something such as a broken heater). In other words, you can drop by and be sympathetic, and they'll allow you in and talk with you.

In my opinion the worst thing that you can do is to berate your tenants from a moral position. Telling them that what they are doing is wrong and evil might make you feel better, but it will likely only make them feel worse and may harden their resolve to avoid doing anything toward making life easier for you.

On the other hand, if you're calm and sympathetic but clear about what you feel you must do, you can sometimes get the action you desire. You can explain that you have your own responsibilities, not the least of which is the mortgage payment. You can point out that you're not the sheriff of Nottingham, but you're not Robin Hood either. You're just a working Joe like them, and this is your business. You simply have to take the action you're taking, or else they will force you out of business. You're only doing what you have to do.

As long as the tenants see you as a person and not a symbol, it's difficult for them to do vile things, such as really trash your place. In addition, they may be inclined to see it your way and work harder to move out. Besides, many tenants simply don't understand what your situation is. They may think you own the property free and clear and could, if you wanted, let them stay there rent-free. Coming to understand how you are being squeezed may help them be more sympathetic to you and less secure in what they are doing. In short, it could motivate them to move.

◆ **CAUTION**   Never appear whiny or weak. If you plead with or beg your tenants, it only undermines your position and makes them think they can take greater advantage of you.

You are there only to explain your position so the tenants will understand you have nothing against them *personally*. Nevertheless, you fully intend to do everything within your rights to get them out. Business, after all, is business.

Explain the Realities of Their Situation

In addition to explaining your position, it can also be very helpful to point out what will happen to the tenants if they continue to refuse to move out. (By the time you start eviction proceedings, you are usually no longer trying as hard to get the tenants to pay up; you just want them out and a different tenant, who pays, in.)

Simply explaining the eviction process itself can be useful. You can point out that they will be served with various papers, that there will be a court hearing and after that, because they have not paid their rent, a judge will order them evicted. At that point the sheriff (or other officer of the court) will come and physically remove them from the property. Their furniture will be picked up by a moving company (which you've paid for) and will eventually be sold.

All of this will be done in addition to their having an eviction on their record. This will be reported (by you) to any local landlords' or housing association, which will then report the fact when future landlords call in to find out about them. It can make it extremely difficult for them to rent another property in the city.

Furthermore, their eviction will be noted by recording services, some of which report to credit agencies. This could affect their credit rating and their ability to get credit, including a home mortgage, in the future.

Finally, once a judgment has been secured against them, the matter of their unpaid rent plus costs will be turned over to a bill collection agency (by you) that will follow them in the future and could garnish wages or take other legal steps to secure the money they haven't paid. (If the problems of eviction are bad for you, they can be doubly bad for the tenant.)

In many cases tenants simply don't know what can happen and think they can just skip out on the rent with impunity. In other cases they may know but don't think you know or simply may not want to face up to the realities. When you point all of this out, it can make a difference. They may decide that peacefully vacating the property is actually to their benefit.

Help the Tenants Move

If reasoning with the tenant works to the point where they seem almost willing to move, it's time to ask the $64 question. "Why can't (or don't) you just move out? After all, it will save both you and me a lot of hassle."

The reasons you get will probably run the gamut from the outrageous to the pitiable. I once had a tenant who wouldn't move out because the astrological signs were not favorable. More likely, however, the tenant may not have a place to move to . . . or may not be able to afford to move.

◆

Smart Landlords Sometimes Help Tenants with Moving Expenses

Sally rented one side of a duplex (dual-living unit) to a couple with two small children. After being there for nearly a year, they said they could no longer pay their rent because the husband, the sole breadwinner, had been laid off. Sally talked to them several times, and they finally confessed that finding a new job in the area (southern California) was hopeless just then. Their only alternative was to move back to Illinois, where the job market was much more favorable.

Sally asked how they would live if they moved. They said they could stay with a relative. The real problem, however, was the moving expenses. They needed to rent a U-Haul truck, which would cost nearly $1,000. But they only had $500.

Sally said she was sympathetic and wanted to help. She offered to pay them the $500 they were lacking, saying they could pay her back sometime in the future, when they had the money. But she would only pay them when they were completely moved out and in the U-Haul, ready to drive away. Within two days they were out and Sally, true to her word, gave them the money.

I'm sure that many of my readers think that Sally was a sap. In truth, she was a very smart landlord. She only lost a few weeks' rent, and the $500 ultimately came from the cleaning/security deposit, which the tenants forfeited. Besides, because of their appreciation for what Sally had done, they did their best to leave the property clean and tidy. As a result, Sally didn't have to spend much at all in cleanup. She got the tenants out, lost virtually no rent (because of the cleaning/security deposit) and only had the usual cleanup to do. What more could a landlord want from a tenant who won't pay and won't move?

Compensate Tenants for Moving

Some would call it a bribe, but I see it as just good business. It's important to always keep your eye on your long-term goals, not just your short-term tactics. You want the property rented to a paying tenant.

If you have a nonpaying tenant there, any legal way you can get that tenant out quickly, at a minimum of expense, is the way to proceed. If it means giving the tenant money, as in the case where Sally helped with the moving costs, so be it. In the long run it was a lot cheaper than a formal eviction. Besides, Sally ended up helping them out; she was a good Samaritan.

Tenant compensation can be in a wide variety of forms. I've known landlords who physically helped tenants load up their furniture, called a distant relative when a tenant was afraid to tell of his or her desperate situation (with the permission of the tenant, of course), helped tenants locate much less expensive rentals, provided dinners and sat until late in the night discussing their options. And I've known landlords who paid tenants off with money to move out; agreed to pay back portions of cleaning/security deposits, regardless of how the property looked when they were out; and paid money for bus tickets to another part of the country. And the stories go on.

Were these landlords being too soft? I don't think so. They were just keeping their eye on the donut and not on the hole. If a little financial or other help can get a tenant out and save a bundle in eviction costs, I feel it's worthwhile.

Landlord's Rule #30

In the long run, a landlord who's pragmatic will make far more money and avoid many more headaches than a landlord who always insists on being right.

Don't Be Afraid To Bite the Bullet

At some point it is time to stop talking and take action. I believe that in the vast majority of cases you can reason with tenants, and a compromise that everyone can live with will eventually be worked out. But not every time.

If you are a landlord long enough, sooner or later you'll come across the tenant who won't move. Nothing you can say or offer will work. This tenant has decided to nest permanently in your property. And from everything you can see, this tenant is also rapidly destroying your property.

In such a case the drastic solution may not only be the best, but it may be the only way out. You may have to legally excise the bad tenant. You may have to absorb the costs, go to court and have the tenant evicted. Then you may have to pay to have your rental unit put back into shape.

I hope it's a long time before this happens to you. But when it happens, the important thing to remember is not to back away from it. I've seen landlords hem and haw because they simply were afraid of eviction. Don't be afraid. Yes, these days it's probably designed more to protect the tenants' rights than yours. But it's the ultimate landlord's tool, when needed.

Landlord's Rule #31

The best way to avoid evicting a tenant is not to rent to him or her in the first place. Nothing takes the place of proper screening of tenants.

16

•••◆•••

When Eviction Is Necessary

Because it is so common and time is of the essence, the eviction process is fairly straightforward and quick in almost all areas of the country. When you seek an eviction, you have priority in terms of court time, and you usually can get a judgment and the eviction in a matter of a few weeks. (But not always, as we'll soon see.)

Experienced landlords know the eviction process quite well but may pick up a few ideas they hadn't considered in this chapter. For those who have not yet or are just now experiencing your first eviction, read closely.

Do You Need an Attorney?

The answer is absolutely yes, the first time anyway. After that, you will have seen how it's done and can probably do it yourself in the future. Most experienced landlords handle their own court evictions and as long as everything goes according to plan, have little trouble doing so.

The biggest question for the new landlord often is, how do you find a good eviction attorney? My suggestion is that you check with local property managers and real estate agents who handle rentals. There usually are one or two attorneys in the county who do nothing but handle evictions. That's their bread and butter. They know all the nuances of the local laws, they know the judges and they know from vast experience what's going to happen and how long it's likely to take.

In addition, eviction attorneys usually have set fees. Sometimes these fees may seem excessive, particularly when you learn how little work is actually involved. However, it's best to learn from an expert, and I think their fees are usually worth it. You should learn enough to be able to handle evictions yourself in the future.

The Eviction Process

The actual eviction process is straightforward. Figure 16.1 summarizes the steps usually taken. Keep in mind that each state has different laws for eviction, which means that time limits and required document filings will differ, sometimes drastically.

The total time in an uncontested eviction shouldn't be much more than four to eight weeks, with six weeks being about average. (Some areas are *much* shorter.) Of course if the eviction is contested, then all bets are off. We'll discuss this later, but first let's consider what many landlords would really like to do with tenants who won't pay and won't quit.

Self-Help Evictions

What should be obvious from the eviction procedure outlined in Figure 16.1 is that it takes time; you lose around six weeks of rent in a simple eviction. And it's costly. There are some court costs to pay, you have to pay an attorney (at least the first time out) and you may have to pay a moving company to collect and store the tenants' furniture. Wouldn't it simply be much easier to get a group of your burly friends, show up one night and throw the tenants out?

This sort of self-help eviction would indeed be simpler; but the trouble is, it isn't legal today. (Around the turn of the century, it was legal almost everywhere in the country!)

FIGURE 16.1 Typical Eviction Procedure

---

1. Serve the initial pay-or-quit notice (3-day, 5-day or whatever).

2. File the unlawful detainer action papers.

3. Serve the eviction papers.

4. Show up in county, municipal or whatever court is appropriate in your area.

5. Tell the story to the judge, and if the tenants don't show, get a judgment to collect the monies owed to you and an eviction.

6. Have final eviction papers with the date of eviction served on the tenants.

7. Have the sheriff or other local law enforcement agency evict the tenants on the designated date. If it gets this far, you will probably have to pay for a local moving company to come and take the tenants' belongings and have them put into storage for later disposition.

8. Have the sheriff give possession of the property back to you.

◆

Hal Gets Lucky with a Self-Help Eviction

A number of years ago, Hal was having a lot of trouble with some tenants in a house he owned. First they were late with the rent. Then they stopped paying altogether. Finally, they wouldn't answer their phone when he called.

Hal was getting frustrated and decided to kick the tenants out. However, when he heard that a local attorney wanted $1,000 to handle the eviction for him, he scoffed and said he would do it himself.

It was the dead of winter, and nights typically dropped well below freezing. Hal showed up one morning at the house and banged on the door until the tenants finally answered. He told them he wanted them out by that afternoon. If they weren't out, he was going to come around with a hammer and break all the windows. (He figured he could get the windows replaced for a lot less than paying an attorney.)

The tenants said that was against the law. If he did that, they would call the sheriff. Hal said they could indeed call the sheriff if they wanted, but by then the windows would be all gone and they'd be sleeping in the cold.

Needless to say, Hal impressed the tenants as being something of a madman, and sure enough, they were out by that evening. Hal congratulated himself on a job well done.

Of course, Hal was just very lucky. If the tenants had been savvy, they might have sued him for threatening them. If they were really savvy, they might have simply stayed and waited. If he carried out his threat, they could have said that one of their children had been injured on broken glass or their furniture had been damaged by rain coming in the broken windows. Perhaps someone had come in and robbed them while the windows were gone. Before the tenants were done, they might have ended up owning the property, and Hal could have been a tenant himself somewhere else.

I mention this story because it's absolutely true and it illustrates about the stupidest thing a landlord can do. The last thing you want is to put yourself in a position where a tenant has good grounds for suing you. In today's litigious society you can be fairly sure that if you try any sort of self-help eviction, you will get caught and it will cost!

◆────────────────────────────────────

Self-Help Actions To Avoid:

- Do not break the windows on the house, remove the doors or anything else that makes the premises uninhabitable.
- Do not turn off the utilities (water, gas, electric, etc.) or plug up the sewer or septic system.
- Do not padlock the tenants out of the property.
- Do not kill their pets or leave gates open so the pets will run loose.
- Do not threaten the tenants.

- Do not disturb their right to quiet enjoyment of the property.
- Do not do anything else that will give the tenants cause to sue you.

Although it might still be condoned in backwoods areas, I personally know of no part of the country that still allows self-help evictions. If you want the tenants out, you go to court.

Landlord's Rule #32

Never, never resort to a self-help eviction of any kind.

Serving Notices

Earlier in this chapter we went through a typical procedure for the legal eviction of tenants. Let's go back now and dwell a bit longer on one aspect of that procedure—serving notices.

The Pay-or-Quit Notice

In almost all areas you must begin the eviction process by serving a pay-or-quit notice. The purpose of this notice is to give tenants written notice that either they must pay the full amount of rent then owed or quit the premises within a specified period of time. The time period varies according to state. In Illinois, for example, it's five days and a 5-day notice is used. California uses a 3-day notice, and tenants have three days to get out or pay. Only after you have served this notice, and tenants have not paid and not quit, can you commence the actual eviction proceeding, usually called an unlawful detainer action.

The pay-or-quit notice usually is presented by a landlord directly to a tenant. Most landlords use it sparingly, since it's sure to alienate tenants. Some use it to get faltering tenants back on track—to let them know you really do mean business. A few landlords hand out these notices as though they were neighborhood flyers. A tenant may be only one day late on the rent and out goes the 3-day notice.

Used sparingly and only when absolutely necessary, the notice can be very effective in spurring a delinquent tenant into performing. Used indiscriminately, such notices can anger perfectly good tenants and result in excessive move-outs.

The notice itself does not have to be in any special form, although it usually should contain the following elements:

- Address of the rental

- Correct names of the tenants

- The total amount due and what period of time this covers

- The time to pay the amount due. (You can give them more time, if you want. The state only sets the minimum time you can give.)

- The date

- Your signature

Figure 16.2 contains a sample notice to pay or quit.

The Notice To Quit

A variation of the pay-or-quit notice is a similar document that does not give a monetary amount. This is used when the tenant has paid the rent but refuses to quit after you have given proper notice asking them to move out. Everything else is essentially the same, except there is no dollar figure on the notice.

Having the Sheriff Serve Notices

After you've served initial notice and the tenants have not quit or paid up the rent, there are now other notices to be served. The number and purpose vary according to your area, but there will be at least two: (1) the initial notice of legal proceedings and (2) the later court-order notice that the tenants must move. There may be intermediate steps as well.

You can serve these notices yourself. However, a better way is to have the local police department or sheriff's office serve the notice. They will do this for what is usually a small fee.

The importance of this, of course, is that when the tenants see the police coming to the door, they are likely to be far more impressed than

---

FIGURE 16.2 3-Day Notice To Pay or Quit

> **CAVEAT** *Portions of the following notice may not apply to your circumstances or may not be legal in your state or area.* **Do not use it or any prewritten form as it is.** *Take it to a competent attorney in your area so that it may be customized for your state and locale and for your particular needs. The author and publisher assume no responsibility for the legality, appropriateness or timeliness of this notice.*

TO:_____

_____

_____

_____

You are hereby notified that the amount of $_____ is now due and payable, representing rent due from ___/___/___ until ___/___/___ for the property described as _____ along with all storage and garage areas.

Demand is hereby made that you pay said rent IN FULL within three (3) days or quit the premises. You are further notified that if you fail to pay or quit, legal proceedings will be instituted against you to terminate your rental agreement or lease, to recover possession of said premises and to recover rents, court costs, attorney fees and damages as specified in your rental agreement or lease.

NO PART PAYMENT OF RENT WILL BE ACCEPTED

Dated this _____day of_____199___

Signed: _____
                   Owner or owner's representative

- -

AFFIDAVIT OF SERVICE

State of _____ County of_____

I, _____, declare under penalty of perjury that I served the above notice on the tenant named above on the _____day of _____, 199___ in the following manner:

FIGURE 16.2   3-Day Notice To Pay or Quit (Continued)

☐ By handing of a copy thereof to the above-named tenant.

☐ By delivering of a copy thereof to _____, a person above the age of 18, residing at the above premises.

☐ By posting a copy thereof in a conspicuous place on the above premises, no one being in actual possession thereof.

☐ By sending a copy thereof by certified mail to the tenant at his place of residence.

State of _____, County ss:

Subscribed and sworn to before me this _____ day of _____ 199__
_____Notary Public

Notary Seal   Signed:_____

---

when they see you coming to the door. A few dollars spent might be just enough to get the tenants to move on their own, allowing you to avoid having to follow through on the entire eviction.

Keep Your Eye on the Goal

This brings us back to the primary goal described in detail in Chapter 15—getting the tenants out. If you're a typical landlord, you're usually not all that interested in going through the entire eviction process. If you can just get the tenants out before it gets to the judge, you can save yourself considerable money in filing fees, attorney costs and additional lost rent.

An exception is if the tenants have assets. If they do, you may want to proceed to get a judgment against them in the hopes of collecting back rent and costs later on down the road.

In most cases, however, tenants who fail to pay rent are judgment-proof. That simply means that they don't have any assets you can attach. In this case, just getting them out quickly is usually your best bet.

Most Tenants Will Move First

Most tenants will simply roll over and play dead when you threaten eviction. They know they haven't paid the rent. They know they are in the wrong. They feel guilty. They act guilty. They are just trying to stall and gain some time.

However, I can only recall fewer than a handful of situations in decades of being a landlord (and being involved with other landlords) where the tenants actually stayed right to the bitter end, and the sheriff had to come and move them out. After all, that's tantamount to having your possessions taken away from you, perhaps never to be seen again. (The tenants can, of course, regain their possessions by paying off costs.) Most sane tenants will move before the date on which this will happen.

Sometimes, however, particularly if there's a nasty divorce involved, the tenants will be unable to act. They will be arguing between themselves even as they are physically evicted.

Tenants Who Contest the Eviction

Thus far we have been discussing an eviction where the tenants do not contest. In some cases, however, savvy tenants will appear in court before the judge and contest the eviction.

If you're a new landlord, you may wonder on what grounds tenants can possibly contest eviction if they haven't paid their rent. (In this discussion we're assuming the eviction is strictly for nonpayment of rent, not because you want them out for other reasons after serving proper notice. The latter case *often* results in a tenant contesting the eviction.) The answer is that at the least, they can claim hardship. At the worst, they can claim that you've done something to them that caused them not to pay rent and that you're to blame.

◆ ———————————————————————————————

Evicting Judgment-Proof Tenants Proves Difficult

Sally rented an apartment to a family with two small children. After staying there nearly six months, they stopped paying rent and refused to move. Nothing she could say or do would change their actions, so she tried eviction.

At the court proceedings, the tenants showed up with their small children. They claimed they had both lost their jobs and were looking for work. They just needed more time. They were particularly worried about their children missing school if they were evicted. Besides, they said they had nowhere to go. The judge gave them a month to come up with the money they owed.

A month later they were back in court. The children were crying, the mother was crying, the father was choked with emotion. They had tried, but they needed more time. The judge gave them another month.

It happened three times for three months. At the end of the third month, they just didn't show, and the judge finally ordered the eviction to take place in three weeks.

Sally served all the papers, of course, but they didn't move . . . until the day before the sheriff showed up along with the moving van Sally had paid for. They were suddenly gone and left the property a mess.

Altogether they were able to stay in the property for four and a half months without paying rent. Since they essentially were judgment-proof, Sally had no real chance of recovering any of her lost costs.

If you want to learn what could happen in a worst-case scenario, then I suggest you rerent the video *Pacific Heights.* Though not aesthetically wonderful, I found the movie absolutely mesmerizing in terms of its portrayal of a "tenant from hell." In the movie an unscrupulous tenant rents an apartment with the specific goal of ruining the owners so that he can take over the building after they cannot afford the mortgage payments and lose the property to foreclosure. Need more be said?

A Caution Regarding Partial Payments

After you begin the eviction process, a tenant may come to you with a partial payment. For example, the tenant may owe five weeks' rent. They may say they don't have the full amount, but they have one week's. They want to give it to you as evidence of their good intention to pay the rest.

Most beginning landlords will take the money on the assumption that one in the hand is worth five in the bush. At least you've got some cash. The problem, however, is that accepting any money at all in part payment from a tenant may corrupt the eviction process. In other words, once you've accepted part payment, if you want to evict the tenant, you may have to start all over again from the beginning with all of the notices. Accepting one week's part payment can set you back a month or more in the eviction process. Be sure to check with an attorney in your state to see what local policy is regarding the acceptance of part rental payment during an eviction.

After the Eviction

Along with the eviction, you will normally also get a judgment for your costs from the court. You can now attempt to trace the former tenants, garnish wages, attach bank accounts and so forth. It's actually an intriguing process, if you have the time and the gumption for it.

A simpler method, and one that often nets better results, is to turn the whole mess over to a collection agency. An agency usually has far more resources than you can muster and probably has both a better chance of tracking down the former tenant as well as getting the cash.

Be aware, however, that most collection agencies work on a percentage basis. Thus, while they may recover the funds, they may keep a third or more for their efforts, depending on the difficulty of getting the money and their policy. Nevertheless, a part of the otherwise lost funds is better than none at all. Collection agencies can be found in the yellow pages of the phone book.

After You Get the Property Back

As soon as the tenants are evicted, secure the premises. That means install new door locks throughout as well as locks on all windows. Immediately begin refurbishing work, particularly on the exterior. Make it quite apparent that someone is taking care of the property. Also, if it's a single-family house, get someone to check on the premises frequently, at least for the first few days. A rental, particularly a separate property, left vacant after an eviction is a prime target for vandalism. A lesser danger is that the former tenants, angered by the eviction, might come back and attempt to do damage to the property. This is probably far less likely, however. In most cases the former tenants are long gone.

Conclusion

Eviction should be a last resort. But when you use it, move quickly and forcefully.

PART FOUR

◆◆◆◆◆◆◆

The Rental as an Investment

17

◆◆◆◆◆◆◆

Raising the Rents

I've never met a landlord who wasn't ready to raise rents. On the other hand, I've also never met one who was willing to lower rents. The conclusion seems to be that from a landlord's perspective, there is only one direction for rents—upward.

Unfortunately, that belies the fact that the rental market in any given area is always changing and not always for the better. Some years it's tight, with more tenants chasing fewer rentals. Other years it's loose, with more landlords chasing fewer tenants. The truth of the matter is that you can only charge what the market will bear. Charge too high a rental rate, and you'll have a vacancy.

As a result, you must watch the market carefully. Sometimes you will actually want to lower your rates to keep a good tenant in a blown market where there are just too many rentals. Do it. You will astonish the tenant and usually avoid the hassle of cleanup and the difficulty of rerenting when there are too many vacancies around.

◆
Lowering the Rent Can Pay Off

A few years ago Hal bought an eight-unit rental property in Phoenix. He had been told that Phoenix was growing at a phenomenal rate, something like 5 percent a year. Yet residential property was amazingly cheap. His plan was simple: buy property, hold it a few years while renting it out and then sell at a profit.

What he didn't realize was that at the time, housing was increasing at well over 5 percent a year. There were far more homes being built than buyers . . . or tenants in the area. In other words, it was a terrible market.

Almost from the moment he bought the property, things began to turn downward. The eight-unit apartment building he bought had been fully rented. But after taking it over, he realized that most of the tenants were nonpaying. The former owner had doctored the books. (See Chapter 18 on taking over a previously owned rental.)

Hal kicked out six nonpaying tenants and then tried to rerent the building. He quickly found that in the highly competitive market, other landlords were offering one or even two months' rent free. Some were offering free TVs or microwaves to anyone who would move in. Others were offering to rent without cleaning or security deposits.

Hal, on the other hand, figured out how much income he would need to cover his expenses, divided by eight and asked that much for each unit. For the two currently occupied units, that meant a rent increase. By the end of the month, the two remaining tenants moved out.

Hal now had a completely empty eight-unit apartment building that stayed empty for five months. At that point he bailed out of the market, selling the building to an investor who just took over for the mortgage amounts. Hal lost his equity. The new investor cut the rental rate, filled up the building and hung onto it for four years, until he eventually sold at a hefty profit.

The moral of this story is simple: You can't always get the rents you want. But you can always get what the market will bear.

How To Determine the Market Rate

Whether you're renting up for the first time or thinking about raising rents, you should always first check out the market. How do you do this?

There are a variety of ways, but the simplest is to look in the local paper where rentals are advertised. Determine the basics first. Is your unit a house, condo or apartment? How many bedrooms and bathrooms does it have? Are there any special amenities, such as a fireplace or pool? (See Chapter 19 for comments on homes with pools.)

Let's say your property is a single-family home with three bedrooms, two baths and a fireplace. Now check out the paper for three bedroom, two bath homes with fireplaces *in the same area as your rental.* It's usually best to do this with the Sunday paper, since more rentals are advertised on Sunday.

Within just a few minutes you can get a good idea of what properties with about the same size, location and features as yours are renting for. If the other property has a pool, deduct a bit from what you can get—e.g., between $50 and $100. If your property has a bigger yard or an extra family room, add a bit. (Check Chapter 19 for comments on houses with big yards.) No, the figures you come up with won't be 100 percent accurate, but they probably will be close to 90 percent accurate.

Now take an afternoon and go to see a half dozen similar rentals in your property's area. Within a very short time, you should be able to get a highly accurate sense of what the market is for your rental. Be sure to ask the landlords how long they've had the house on the market and if there are any reductions, for example, for signing a year's lease. This should give you a good place to start in determining how much rent you can charge for your property.

Another method is to call several local real estate agents whose offices specialize in the management of rentals. Describe your property. (You can say you're considering using a property management firm, which you may very well be doing. See Chapter 21.) They usually will be happy to send someone over to tell you what they think you can get in rent. Check with three or four firms, and you'll have an extremely accurate estimation of your optimum rental rate. These experts also can quickly let you know if there are any move-in bonuses that are common in your area, such as gifts, free rent, etc.

Yet another method is to join the local rental property owners' association, if there is one in your area. These organizations can give you lists of rental rates as well as provide leases and other forms most suited to your area.

Thus, with a day or two of work, you should be able to quickly and easily determine the market rental rate for your unit.

Landlord's Rule #33

You can't always rent for what you need to make your monthly payments. But you can always rent for what the market will bear.

Don't Be Stubborn When It Comes to the Market

Your property will rent for whatever amount the market will bear, and that has no relation to what your expenses are. For example, it may cost you $1,000 a month for mortgage payments, taxes, insurance, maintenance and so on. But the market may only allow you to rent your property for $500 a month or $1,500 a month.

One of the greatest mistakes a landlord can make is to try to fight the market. You want $750 a month, but the market will only bear $700. So you stubbornly hold out for your money. Eventually, four months later, you find some crazy tenant who's willing to pay your rate, and you exult at your victory. But have you won or lost?

Consider that it took you four months to find this crazy tenant. That's $2,800 in lost rent that you presumably would have received by renting immediately at the market rate of $700 a month. But, of course, you're now getting $50 a month more, a rate of $750. The problem is that it will take you 56 months, more than four years, to recoup the lost four months of rent. Renting immediately for $700, you might have been able to raise the rents $50 a month after one year.

Landlord's Rule #34

It's a lot worse to have a property vacant than to have it rented full-time at a lower rate than you want.

Your goal is to get as close to 100 percent occupancy as possible. If you drop below 90 percent occupancy, you're probably charging too high a rental rate.

When To Raise Rents

Some landlords have a rule of thumb that goes like this. They raise the rents every year the tenant stays in the property. It's kind of like a penalty for renting from them. The longer the tenant stays, the more the tenant has to pay. However, with these landlords tenants rarely stay long.

In my opinion there are three conditions that must be in effect before you raise the rents. They are as follows:

1. You must have more money from the rental. If you're in a negative cash flow situation, you probably won't survive long holding on to the property. Either you won't have the funds to continue or your will to stick it out will be worn down. Any rental property worth its salt should at the least break even. (That's after all considerations, including extra rental income from washing machines, Coke machines, extra car spaces and so on, as well as all write-offs, including depreciation.)

You have to raise the rents. Of course, you have to be able to get an increased rental amount.

2. The market will bear an increase. You've done your homework and found out what other rentals are charging. You are charging less. You probably will be able to sustain a rental increase.

3. The tenants will feel you are justified in raising rates. Your goal is not to have the tenants move out. Instead, keep the same tenants, only get a higher rental rate. To accomplish this, the tenants must feel that you are justified in raising rates. They will feel you are justified if you handle the increase in a civilized manner (with respect for their feelings); present a logical case, including a market analysis of other rental rates; and assure them that there won't be another increase very soon. When they check it out and discover that you're correct, they'll probably stay.

The Cost-of-Moving Factor

You should be aware that tenants almost always consider the cost of moving. If you are charging the current market rate, you can often successfully raise the rents a bit more, depending on what it costs for the tenants to move someplace else. For example, let's say the typical costs of moving are $1,000. You might successfully raise the rent $50 a month on a year's lease even though that's $50 higher than the market rate. Over a year it only comes to $600, less than the cost of moving someplace else.

Landlord's Rule #35 _____

Don't overlook the inertia factor. Most people don't like to move. It's a hassle. The kids might have to change schools. As a result, your tenants may stay simply because it's easier than moving. Of course, increase the rents high enough and you'll drive any tenant out.

18

◆◆◆◆◆◆

The Insurance You Need

There's an old maxim about insurance that goes something like this: No matter how much insurance you buy, when you have a claim, chances are you're not going to be covered for your specific loss. I suppose the reasoning behind this stems from the fact that insurance companies are hesitant to write coverage for areas in which they are likely to suffer loss. That's why it's hard to get flood insurance next to rivers, earthquake insurance on faults and fire insurance in the woods. Of course, those are just the places you need the coverage the most!

Nevertheless, insurance is usually available to landlords, and generally (but not always) the limits and rates are not unreasonable. In this chapter we will examine some of the insurance needs that you as a landlord may have to consider.

Getting the Most Liability Insurance

For a moment, ask yourself what is the worst thing that's likely to happen to you as a landlord. Is it having the house burn down? Is it not being able to find tenants to rent up the premises? Is it having a tenant leave the property a mess?

I maintain that although the chances are very slim, the worst that could happen to you is to have a tenant sue you—for example, for injury on your property—and you are not fully covered by insurance. Your property might only be worth $150,000, but you could be liable for hundreds of thousands of dollars or more in damages. This applies whether you own the property or are managing it for someone else. (You can be assured that in any suit both the owner and the landlord—if they are different—will be named.) Therefore, it behooves you to carry full liability insurance. This will cover you for many things related to a property, and for which you can be sued.

Landlord's Rule #36

The only way to guarantee that you won't need insurance coverage is to carry it.

Thus, the question becomes not whether or not you should have liability insurance, but how much to carry. Many property management firms say that you should carry between $300,000 and $500,000 in liability insurance. I think their reasoning stems from the fact that many insurance companies today limit the liability coverage you can get on a single-family rental property to those amounts.

However, umbrella policies that cover excess liability are available from many companies. They take over when your regular liability insurance ends and goes on up. A few years ago I was involved with a condominium rental project that had over 100 units, and we regularly carried a minimum of $15 million in liability insurance.

Although liability premiums are constantly rising, the point to remember is that after you pay your basic premium for the $300,000 or $500,000 or whatever, the umbrella excess coverage is actually quite cheap. I believe the insurance companies reason that their risk is greatest for the first $100,000 and decreases dramatically after that. Maybe so, but I suggest you let them worry about statistical risk. To sleep well at night, I prefer an umbrella that reaches into the millions.

Fire Insurance

If you have a mortgage on your property, you almost certainly are required to carry, at minimum, basic fire insurance. This simply means that if the building burns down, your lender gets paid.

However, you should carry enough fire insurance so that you can have your interest in the building protected as well. In other words, you want your equity saved.

In the old days insurance companies only offered a form of insurance that would pay a cash settlement amount. For example, you would insure your property for $100,000, and that's what you would get if the building burned down. If you owed $80,000, the lender would get that money and you'd get the remainder, or $20,000.

Today, however, most insurance polices involve some sort of replacement cost. In other words, if your building burns down, the insurance company will make the mortgage payments for a period of time (usually up to one year) and will rebuild the property so that you are back where you started. (Except, of course, that you end up with a brand-new building instead of an older one.)

If all this sounds terrific, be aware that there are many pitfalls along the way.

Replacement Cost Insurance

To get replacement cost insurance, you must buy it. If your policy doesn't specifically say you have it, you may not. Check with your insurance agent.

Be aware that there are two types of replacement cost insurance—standard and guaranteed. Under the standard form your property is depreciated, and you only get the depreciated value, which may not be enough to actually replace it. Under the guaranteed form the insurance company replaces your property, often regardless of the cost. Guaranteed replacement cost has only recently become available on rental properties from many insurance companies.

Amount of Insurance Coverage

As a condition of your mortgage, virtually all lenders will require that you carry a *minimum* amount of fire insurance. Typically, they will want you to carry enough to cover the mortgage amount. That, however, may actually be too much coverage!

Today, in parts of the country where real estate values are high, a significant portion of the cost of a piece of property is the land value. In some cases the land values may be 50 percent or more of the total property value. The thing about land, however, is that it doesn't burn. So why insure it? Because the lender demands it.

For example, you want to buy a property worth $300,000, of which the land is worth $150,000. When you purchase the property, you get an 80 percent mortgage, or $240,000. Naturally enough, the lender wants you to carry $240,000 worth of fire insurance. That's unrealistic, however, since your building's value is only $150,000. Rest assured that the premium on that extra $90,000 will cost you a pretty penny. But what can you do if you want to get the loan?

◆
Landlord's Hint

If you get guaranteed replacement cost insurance, in many states the lender is prohibited from demanding that you carry the full mortgage amount. It only makes sense. The insurer guarantees to replace the building in the event of a fire, so there's no risk to the lender. In our example, the insurance amount with guaranteed replacement shouldn't be for more than $150,000. Check with an insurance agent in your state to see if this applies where you live.

Extended or Homeowner's Insurance

If you own and live in your own home, in addition to the standard form of fire insurance, you may also purchase homeowner's insurance. This covers you for a large number of risks in addition to fire, often including damage caused by storms, aircraft crash, smoke, burst pipes (not the pipes, but the damage caused by the water), vandalism, falling trees, landslides and much more. In the past this type of coverage was not always available to rental property owners.

Today, however, extended coverage for rentals is available from many insurers, and the cost is often only a fraction of the cost over and above the standard policy. It's like getting homeowner's insurance (albeit not quite as good) for a rental. My suggestion is that you definitely carry this extra coverage.

Earthquake, Flood and Storm Endorsements or Policies

In California you want earthquake insurance. In parts of the Midwest you need flood insurance. In Florida and along the Gulf Coast it's hurricane insurance.

If you are in a high-risk area, chances are that this kind of insurance is not available through the normal channels. Most insurance companies simply won't cover the risk at any cost. However, there may be pooled risk insurance available, or the federal or state government may offer insurance (such as the Federal Flood Program), often at very reasonable cost. Check with a good insurance agent.

On the other hand, insurance companies handle many areas that are subject to these sorts of natural calamities but are not in high-risk areas. For example, in most parts of California you can still get earthquake insurance, either as an endorsement to your fire insurance policy or as a separate policy.

The price when offered is often fairly reasonable. If for no other reason, you may want to purchase this insurance just for your piece of mind.

◆ **CAUTION**   Earthquake, flood and storm insurance often have strict limitations. They may have very high deductibles, perhaps as high as 5 or 10 percent of the policy amount, and the total coverage may be limited. Furthermore, unless you insure with a very large company, a major storm or flood could wipe out an insurance company's reserves, meaning that you might only get part payment.

Other Coverage To Consider

In addition to the types of coverage just mentioned that are usually associated with a fire insurance policy, there are other risks that you may want to consider. A good policy should cover all of these risks, though not necessarily. If they aren't covered, ask your agent about adding them in, or check with a different insurer who does offer them.

Vandalism. Usually covered under an extended fire insurance policy, this is becoming increasingly more important. Today one vandal with a can of spray paint can do thousands of dollars of damage to your property in a few minutes. Broken windows, break-ins and other forms of vandalism are also increasing. You should have insurance to cover you against these threats.

Inflation Guard. This automatically ups the value of your insurance annually and is usually based on some index, such as the Consumer Price Index. The idea here is that the same property costs more to replace each year. With this coverage you shouldn't unexpectedly find that you aren't fully insured due to inflation.

Demolition and Code Upgrade. When you have a loss, your property will often only be partially destroyed (although it may be a total economic loss). That means that someone must bulldoze the wreck. Unless you have a special demolition endorsement, this may not be covered by your policy.

Similarly, if you have an older property, the building code in your area may have been upgraded since your rental was built. It may cost more to replace your property today simply because the newer building codes are stricter. This type of endorsement pays the additional cost of reconstruction due to changes in building codes.

Loss of Rents. Although this is added in to most extended coverage policies, you'll want to check to be sure it's in yours. This type of coverage guarantees that while your property is uninhabitable because of fire or other calamity, you get paid your rents as if it were fully occupied. This allows you to continue making your mortgage and other payments.

Glass Breakage, Furniture Coverage and Other Endorsements.
Don't automatically assume that all your glass is covered in your policy. There may be a deductible that's fairly high as well as a maximum amount covered. These limits can be changed by a special endorsement. The same holds true for furniture or other personal property that you

may own on the property, such as washers and dryers, heaters and boilers, appliances, snowblowers and so on.

◆ **CAUTION**   In the past insurance companies protected you during the period of coverage regardless of when a claim was made. For example, let's say you bought a policy from XYZ Insurance in 1992, kept it for one year and then switched to ABC Insurance in 1993. Then in 1994 a former tenant sued you for something that happened back in 1992. Although you were no longer with XYZ insurance, in years past it would nevertheless honor the coverage because the claim occurred while you were covered.

Today, however, in many states insurers no longer have to honor claims *after* they stop insuring the property, even if the claims relate to a time when they did have the coverage. This is usually called claims-made insurance and refers to the fact that the insurance company only pays for claims made during the insured period.

Since there is a statute of limitations in most states for filing claims, however, you will probably want coverage that extends forward for several years, which requires a special endorsement. On the other hand, your current policy may also be a claims-made policy that will handle claims currently filed even if the occurrence was before the policy took effect. Check carefully into your policy and with your agent to see what you have and what you may need to get.

Of course there are other endorsements available for almost any type of risk. The best bet is to find a good insurance agent and let him or her go over your property concerns with you. You may find you need much more coverage . . . or much less!

Tenant's Insurance

Many new landlords are surprised to discover that their extended coverage policy doesn't cover the personal property of tenants. If there's a broken pipe, for example, and some of the tenants' furniture is destroyed, your policy may not cover it. This, however, would only encourage the tenants to sue you for damages because of the broken pipe.

◆ **CAUTION**   In the past it was usually necessary for a tenant to show negligence on the landlord's part to win a lawsuit involving a rental. Increasingly, however, the tenants only have to show that there's a defect in the property. This could have important consequences for you if your tenants are injured or their possessions are damaged.

Tenant's insurance, however, provides a way for tenants to cover their belongings. It's widely available and is roughly the kind of insurance you get with a homeowner's policy. Extended fire policies are available that usually protect tenants from a wide variety of risks—from fire to dog bites.

Landlord's Rule #37

When they move in, always tell your tenants that their belongings are *not* covered under your insurance policy. Encourage them to get their own tenant's policy.

Workers' Compensation

Workers' compensation pays a worker when he or she is injured on the job. But, you may say, you aren't hiring anyone, so why do you need workers' compensation?

The answer is that you may hire an independent contractor to do anything from mow your lawn to fix your roof. Presumably, that independent contractor carries workers' compensation. But if he or she doesn't and someone is injured on the job, you can almost be certain that the injured person will come to you for compensation. It's at that point that your workers' compensation should cut in.

In some states workers' compensation is required to be included on all broad coverage insurance. In others, it isn't, so be sure to check your policy and with your agent to see what kind of coverage you have. If you don't have workers' compensation, I strongly urge you to get it. The premium is typically not very high for a landlord (or property owner) when added to an extended policy and is usually well worth the expense.

Home Warranty Insurance

These days whenever you buy a house or condo, the real estate agents virtually plead with you to get home warranty insurance. This protects you (and them) against a whole host of problems in the property, from leaky water heaters to broken furnaces. The insurance typically costs between $200 and $300 and is usually paid for by the seller.

This insurance is also sometimes available for rental property. And once in place, it can often be extended year-to-year by the landlord/owner.

Why would you want to pay around $250 a year for home warranty insurance? If you have a relatively new property, you probably wouldn't. But if you have an older property, one in which you are having problems with the heating, electrical or plumbing systems or something else involving big costs, this insurance could literally save you thousands a year. (The cost of one heat exchanger in a gas furnace, for example, might pay for three or four years of insurance.)

There are two problems, however. First, in order to get the insurance initially, the seller must sign a statement that says that all the home appliances and systems are in good working order. Most sellers are hesitant to sign such a statement unless it's completely true for fear the insurance company will come after them if something turns out to have been broken.

Second, it's much harder to get home warranty insurance if no sale is involved. Yes, it is available, but the insurance companies tend to be far more suspicious, as they wonder if there's some problem with the property that's causing you to seek out the insurance.

When available and for the right property, this insurance can be just plain wonderful.

Finding the Right Insurance Company

There was a time when you could have your choice of dozens of insurance companies that were willing to take your premiums and give you insurance for all the risks you wanted to cover. However, that's changed in the last few years. With a host of natural catastrophes blanketing the nation—from hurricanes in Florida to floods in the Midwest to fires and earthquakes in California—some insurance companies have been forced out of business by enormous claims while others, even the biggest, have been forced to cut back. Today you may find that there is only a handful of insurers available, or in some cases none at all!

The result is that you may not have a chance to pick and choose just the right insurer for you. If that's the case, you simply must take what you can get. But if you do have the happy option of selecting between several insurers, here are a few points to watch out for:

- *Ratings.* Insurance companies are rated by several firms, probably the most well known of which is Best. Go for an insurance company with a Best rating of at least A and preferably A+.

- *Agents.* Check out the agents. Some are independents and can give you quotes from a variety of companies, such as Cigna or Travelers. Others write only for one company, such as State Farm or Allstate. Obtain several quotes and compare the cost against what you get. And be sure that you're covered! You should demand proof of coverage when you pay your premium, else the agent might delay sending in your policy and if catastrophe strikes too soon, you might not have coverage.

- *Deductibles.* Consider deductibles carefully. Many companies will offer significantly reduced premiums for higher deductibles. For example, you might cut your policy cost in half if you accept a $1,000 deductible as opposed to a $100 deductible. But, you may argue, think of the $900 you could lose in the event of a claim!

  That's exactly what I am thinking about. By accepting a higher deductible, you are in effect self-insuring your property. And this may be a good idea. Say you have a claim for $800. You have a $100 deductible and you turn the claim in, the insurance company pays off and you get $700. But the next time your premium comes along, it may go up. Or you may find that your insurer really doesn't want your business any more.

On the other hand, say you have a $1,000 deductible and you pay the $700 claim yourself. You don't turn it in to your insurance company. Now you have the benefits of a lower premium, and your insurer loves you because you haven't had any claims.

The point here is that you end up paying either way. However, with a higher deductible and self-insurance for small claims, you may save money in the long run and end up with a better insurer and a better policy.

Look for Premium Savers

Most insurance companies offer reduced premiums for certain types of equipment. For example, if you have a smoke detector in the property (often a mandatory requirement of your building and safety code), your premium may be reduced. Similarly, there may be reductions for fire extinguishers kept on the property and sprinkler or security alarm systems. Check with your insurance company to see how you can save.

Be Careful with Claims

I have a cynical friend who says that the entire purpose of many insurance companies is to collect premiums and deny claims. Don't expect your insurance company to instantly take your word for everything and pay off what you want. You need to document any occurrences, particularly those that involve injury. (Of course, be sure that the injured party immediately receives appropriate medical care.)

Get statements from witnesses, if appropriate. Keep the invoices for all work you have done. Pay by check, and when you get your cancelled check back from the bank, hang onto it as proof that you paid for the work done. (Yes, there still are banks today that will send back cancelled checks, if you demand it!) Keep a diary, if possible, recounting all incidents. And report claims promptly to your insurer.

Note: You may also want to look into a *personal adjuster,* one who works for you, especially for larger losses. Look in the Yellow Pages under adjusters.

19

◆◆◆◆◆◆◆

The Involuntary Landlord

Most of us choose to be landlords. But sometimes handling a rental property is thrust upon us, perhaps when we least want the responsibility. We may have a nice cozy life just going in and out of work each day, and all of a sudden we're in charge of the routine of finding tenants, cleaning up and collecting rents. How can this happen involuntarily?

It's really quite simple and has probably occurred with more frequency over the past five years than over the previous 50. An industry phases out and a job disappears, so a homeowner suddenly has to move. But the homeowner can't resell in the current depressed real estate market. Renting out the property suddenly seems the only viable alternative, and the homeowner now becomes an involuntary landlord.

◆

Jimmy Suddenly Becomes a Landlord in a Weak Market

Jimmy was living in southern California and worked in an aerospace firm. Suddenly he was laid off.

He immediately put out feelers and landed a job in Arizona. He put his current home up for sale and prepared to move. The trouble was that everyone else was in his boat. There were over 750,000 people laid off in southern California between 1990 and

1993, and you can bet that almost every one of them wanted to sell his or her house.

As a result, prices were falling and houses weren't selling. So Jimmy was faced with two home payments, one for the house he owned in southern California and another for the house he was renting for his family in Arizona. He just couldn't handle that, so he decided to become a landlord and rent out the southern California house.

Now he's worried. What is he up against? What are his chances of succeeding?

How To Determine If You Will Succeed at Being an Involuntary Landlord

Thus far we've discussed what's involved in handling the actual renting of property. If you're worried that you might not have the stomach for it, just reread the first chapters of this book. They will give you a good idea of what you're up against.

If you decide that taking care of even just one property is too much, read Chapter 21, which explains what's involved in hiring a property management firm. Perhaps a management firm can handle any unpleasantness for you.

However, beyond the personality requirements for being a landlord, there are also property requirements. To the surprise of some investors, not all properties make good rentals. Some should *never* be rented out. Before you become an involuntary landlord, therefore, give serious consideration to how well your property will fare.

Is Your Property Suitable as a Rental?

Can't every property be rented out, you might ask?

Every property certainly can be rented, at some price and at some risk of damage. The problem is that some properties command smaller rental rates and offer greater risks. Let's look at some of the concerns.

The House with a Pool

You may think that a pool is a great advantage. When I initially started purchasing properties as rentals, I thought it was a big plus. A pool meant I could always get more rent.

However, there are a growing number of homeowners and now landlords who realize that the problems a swimming pool produces often far and away exceed the benefits. Thus, in many markets a pool is not a plus but at best a "wash" and at worst a negative feature. Nevertheless, in Sun Belt states you can often rent out a home with a pool more quickly and for more money than a home without one, probably in the neighborhood of $50 to $100 more.

However, in my opinion, a pool is always a negative for rentals, even with the increased revenue and the speedier rent-up time it brings. Here are several reasons why.

Liability.   Adults, children, dogs and cats sometimes have accidents in and around pools. Fortunately, drownings tend to be at a minimum. But people falling in, skinning their knees or other parts on tiles, injuring themselves while diving and so on happens far more often than most of us realize. When we own a home with a pool, we can watch to be sure that adverse things such as these don't occur. When we rent out, however, it's up to the tenants to be careful. And if they're not careful, we may be asked to pay the price.

To protect yourself from charges of negligence, at a minimum you will need to have a fence that completely surrounds the yard where the pool is. Even in an enclosed backyard, it's better to have a second fence just surrounding the pool itself to ensure that a small child can't wander out of the back door of the house and accidentally fall in.

When I had pool home rentals, I also always removed all diving boards, slides and other accessories that actually make the pool more fun. There's simply too much danger of someone being injured on them.

Finally, you'll want to have adequate liability insurance. Many property management firms suggest a minimum of $300,000 to $500,000. I recommend a minimum of $3 million through a combination of standard liability insurance and an umbrella policy. (See Chapter 18.) The trouble is that in some areas it's difficult to get this kind of insurance for a rental.

Cost.   No matter what anyone says, pools are not cheap. Besides extra insurance, they require large amounts of electricity to run the pump and chemicals to maintain the water purity. Depending on the condition of your pool, the costs can be anywhere from $15 to $150 a month, offsetting much of the increase in rental income the pool might bring in.

Upkeep.   Someone has to clean the pool, clean the filter, put in the chemicals and so forth. A pool service can easily cost $100 a month. And don't make the mistake of thinking you can have your tenants handle the upkeep. Tenants are notoriously forgetful when it comes to remembering to add the appropriate chemicals and clean the pool regularly. Besides, do you really want the liability that comes when a tenant pours chemicals such as acid and chlorine into the water and accidentally burns himself or herself?

Repairs.   Pools don't repair themselves. You must hire someone to fix pump motors and clogged filters. Broken or clogged pipes, black algae growing into plaster and cracks in the cement are just a few of the very expensive costs that can occur, particularly when you're not there to watch out for the pool yourself.

In short, because pools are a liability problem, are difficult and expensive to maintain and have all sorts of costly physical problems, *my feeling* is that a house with a pool is simply not suitable for renting out. It's better for you to sell it now at a loss than rent it out and have to pay thousands of dollars because of the pool later on.

I realize, of course, that many property managers may scoff at such concerns. Many, in fact, do successfully rent out houses with large pools. I only offer that their experiences have been different from mine. In my book, a pool automatically disqualifies a property from rental status.

The Very Old House

Houses, in one sense, are like cars; they deteriorate over time. When a house is new—i.e., under seven years of age—usually nothing or at most very little goes wrong. By the time it's a teenager, however, important areas begin causing trouble, such as water heaters, roofs and appliances. As a house gets into its twenties and thirties, there are additional problems with the heating/air-conditioning system and plumbing, and walls and ceilings being to crack from a settling foundation. A house that reaches the ripe old age of 40, however, can need replacement of the entire plumbing system (converting from rusting galvanized steel to copper) and electrical system (converting from a two-wire to a three-wire grounded system) in addition to complete roof replacement, foundation repair, driveway replacement and so on.

Yes, it's true that these expenses may occur whether you're living in the property or renting it out. However, when you are living there, you can "nurse it along," making do with old and decrepit features. But when you're renting out, you must be sure that the property is habitable and that it meets minimum public health and safety standards (unless, of course, you want your specialty to become that of slumlord, a topic not covered in this book). When the air-conditioning or heating systems fail, the tenant wants them fixed immediately, and that usually means complete replacement. On the other hand, if you are living in the property, you might wear a bathing suit in summer or an extra sweater in winter for a few weeks until a less expensive repair part can be found. The same holds true for leaking roofs, electrical systems that fail, plumbing that stops up and so forth. No tenant will tolerate what you might tolerate. The result of all of this is that maintenance and repair costs mean it's more expensive to rent out an older house.

Again I recognize that many colleagues disagree. In particular I recall a column by the excellent syndicated writer Robert Bruss, in which he pointed out that a well-maintained, well-located older home could do very well as an investment rental.

He is, of course, correct. If there are no or minimal physical or location problems with a house of any age, it should be a good rental opportunity. He has obviously had good experiences with them. However, my own personal experience with many older properties has been that sooner or later they give me very expensive headaches.

The Poorly Located House

Everyone knows that location is the most important aspect of real estate. What few realize, however, is that a great location for a home to buy or sell doesn't necessarily make for a great home to rent.

Properties that are close to work sites, shopping, bus lines and so on usually make good rentals. On the other hand, their proximity to such services may make it more difficult to sell the house.

On the other hand, a house located far out in the woods may be an idyllic setting for someone buying a home and wanting a romantic location. But a renter may not want the hassle of a long drive and the upkeep of a woodsy location.

In general, single-family homes, apartments, condos, duplexes and almost all other kinds of residential rental property do best as rentals in an urban or suburban setting that is clean, relatively crime free and newer. Houses that are far out, that are in high-crime areas or that have difficult access to freeways or bus routes, do less well.

The High-Maintenance House

As a homeowner, you may be willing to spend several hours a week watering the lawns and shrubs. I can almost guarantee that your tenants won't bother. If your house has automatic sprinklers, drip or other watering systems, it's a big plus as a rental. If everything has to be done manually, however, it's a minus.

Big yards are great for big families, particularly when you live in the property. But if you're renting it out, big yards attract big families, which means extra wear and tear on your property. There's also the matter of who is going to mow the lawns, trim the shrubs and rake the leaves.

Houses with big yards tend to be a minus for landlords. Either you're going to be fighting the tenants to get the work done or you'll have to hire a gardening service, which can cost a substantial amount of money. (Hiring a gardening service, however, is a plus when finding a tenant and often allows you to charge a slightly higher rent—rarely, however, high enough to pay for the entire gardening service.) Houses with big yards also tend to be costly in terms of water.

Landlord's Rule #38

Try to avoid converting your residence to a rental if it has a pool, is old and run down, is far off the beaten track or has a high-maintenance yard. If you do convert with these negative features, you may end up with a substantial negative cash flow on the property.

What If Your Property Isn't Suitable as a Rental?

From the previous discussion you should be able to get a fairly good idea of your chances of commanding a reasonably good rent without a lot of hassle for your property when you convert it from your personal residence to a rental. If, however, it is a poor rental risk, you might be better off seeking an alternative to renting. What, you may ask, is the alternative?

There are a variety of alternatives for people who must move and don't want to become a landlord. They are as follows:

- *Sell out at a loss.* Sometimes it's better to bite the bullet and get on with your life. In the years ahead you can earn back the money you lose. Besides, without the headache of the house, you might live longer!

- *If housing prices have really fallen since your purchase (in a worst-case scenario you owe more than the mortgage), negotiate with the lender.* In a really bad market the last thing a lender wants is another foreclosure. As of this writing, many people in southern California (currently a very depressed market) are getting lenders to agree to accept as loan payoffs whatever the market price is for their house, even if it's less than the loan amount! Of course, not all lenders are agreeable, but it doesn't hurt to try.

- *If you decide to stick it out, consider taking in a partner.* Advertise for someone who wants ownership but who can't qualify for a loan or make a big down payment. If they can make a rental payment high enough to pay your expenses, work out an agreement with them in which you'll share the profits of a future sale if they will stay in the property and make payments. Called an equity-sharing arrangement, a good real estate lawyer can create the appropriate documents to make it work.

For more alternatives, I suggest checking into two books, *Buy, Rent and Hold,* available from McGraw-Hill, and *How to Sell Your Home in a Down Market,* available from Warner Books, both by my favorite author, me.

Landlord's Rule #39

When converting isn't advisable, try selling the property or taking in an equity-sharing partner.

Tax Consequences of Renting Out Your Personal Residence

It's important to understand that the tax treatment of a personal residence is significantly different from the tax treatment of a rental property. When you convert from a personal residence to a rental property, you may give up some tax advantages.

◆ **CAUTION**   It's beyond the scope of this book to detail the tax consequences of conversion from personal residence to rental. You should check with your tax adviser. You may also want to read *Tips and Traps for Saving on ALL of Your Real Estate Taxes* by Robert Irwin and Norman Lane (McGraw-Hill, 1994) or *The Real Estate Investor's Tax Guide* by Vernon Hoven (Real Estate Education Company, 1993). Here I provide an overview of some tax consequences. It is not complete, however, and may or may not apply to your circumstances.

One of the most important tax advantages of selling a principal residence is that you can roll over your taxable gain into a new home, provided you meet certain guidelines that include buying the new residence within four years (two years before or after the sale of the old home) and paying more for the new home than the old. (Even if you pay less for the new property, some of the taxable gain can be rolled over.) Furthermore, when you reach the age of 55, you have a once-in-a-lifetime exclusion of up to $125,000 in taxable gain, again providing you meet strict guidelines. Both of these advantages, however, apply only to a principal residence, not to a rental.

A big question for many inadvertent landlords, therefore, is how do I maintain the tax advantages of a principal residence when I am forced to temporarily rent out my property? This is a gray area, and there are no hard-and-fast rules. However, generally speaking, if the rental period doesn't exceed two years (the time before or after selling a principal residence that you have to replace it with a new property), you can probably still roll over the sale. This probably also applies to the $125,000 exclusion since one of the requirements is that the property was owned and used as your principal residence for three out of the past five years. Again, check with a tax specialist first.

Tax Losses

When you rent out your property, you may be able to take deductions, including depreciation, and even show a tax loss. Any tax loss on a rental, however, is subject to the active/passive rules that may limit your ability to write off the loss against your personal income if that income exceeds $100,000. This is a complex subject and is beyond the scope of this book. Again, consult *Tips and Traps for Saving on ALL of Your Real Estate Taxes* by Irwin and Lane and your tax adviser.

Additionally, if you use the home part of the year as your residence and part as a rental, certain vacation home rules may come into play, and this also could restrict (or enhance) your ability to write off deductions.

Finally, be aware that the IRS has denied some deductions on homes where the intent was to only temporarily convert them to rentals. In this case, you could only deduct expenses to the extent of your rental income. This ruling, however, has been successfully challenged in court. This is definitely a subject for your tax attorney.

20

♦♦♦◆♦♦♦

Taking Over a Rental Property

Some people think that taking over an existing rental filled with tenants is a plus. Let's say you buy a six-unit apartment building that is fully leased. You don't have to worry about finding tenants; you just sit back and collect the rents, right?

Maybe! Depending on how careful you were in your purchase, the terms of your sales contract and your own investigative efforts, you could have purchased anything from a nightmare to a gold mine. In this chapter we will consider some of the ramifications of buying preleased properties.

Who's Got the Deposits?

This is probably the biggest area of conflict. Chances are that every tenant in the property you're buying paid a deposit(s) to the former owner of some amount for some purpose. But how big was the deposit and who now has the money?

If you're taking on a large property—say, 100 rental units—and the deposits were $750 apiece, you're talking about $75,000. That's serious money, not something you leave to chance. Even if it's just a single-family house that's rented out, there could be $1,000 or more in deposit money somewhere. If you wait until *after* you make the purchase to go after the money, you may never find it and may indeed be responsible for ultimately paying it back out of your own pocket. The time to track it down is beforehand.

Who Has the Last Month's Rent?

The same holds true for the last month's rent. If the property is leased, chances are the tenant(s) has paid a last month's rent up front. The old landlord got the money. But unless it's placed into escrow or otherwise handled as part of your purchase transaction, you may never see it.

◆───────────────────────────────────────

Sally Gets Tough on Deposits and Last Month's Rent

Sally was purchasing a 14-unit apartment house that was almost fully rented (one unit was vacant). She had a clause inserted in the sales agreement that said that the seller was to turn over to her all deposits and last months' rents and furthermore, that she had the right to secure an inventory of the funds. However, the seller said there were no deposits and all the tenants were on a month-to-month basis, none having paid a last month's rent; hence, there was nothing to turn over. Although he had signed rental agreements with all of them, he could not produce any deposits. He said they had somehow been misplaced.

So Sally went door-to-door in the building, introducing herself as the person who was buying the property and asking the tenants about rental agreements, deposits and last months' rents. Surprisingly, nearly all of the tenants had copies of their rental agreements. She found that five of the tenants had leases and had paid the last month's rent up front. Furthermore, all of them claimed to have put up cleaning/security deposits of one kind or another. As the new owner, she would be responsible for one day returning those funds.

Sally inventoried the monies and then presented her inventory to the seller. It came to over $12,000. She said that the money was owed to her in cash, as part of the deal. The seller said, "No way!" He at first disputed the claims of the tenants about deposits and last months' rents and then said that they had indeed put up money, but it was a much lower figure. In any event, he said he had spent it all and wasn't about to sweeten the sale by $12,000. Sally pointed out that he was obligated to come up with the money, or they had no deal. After all, she wasn't going to pay $12,000 extra for the property just because he had taken the deposits and last month's rents and spent them.

They eventually reached a compromise—part cash and part better terms on a mortgage the owner was carrying back. Sally got her building and took care of the deposits and the last months' rents.

This story illustrates a way to handle deposits and last months' rents when buying an occupied rental property. Of course, you can always buy blind and take your chances later on. However, as noted earlier in this book, with very expensive properties the combined deposits and other funds held for tenants can sometimes be as large or larger than the purchase down payment! It's not something you want to just let go.

Giving Notice of a Change in Ownership

After the purchase it's important to formally let the tenants know that you're the new owner and to inform them of the way you intend to do business. I have found that the best way to accomplish this is by a formal letter. Ideally, you would have a sign-off letter from the former landlord (required in some states) and a sign-on letter from you, the new landlord. This will let the tenants know what's happening and reassure them that there is a continuity of management and that their interests are protected.

The old landlord's letter need only be short and sweet. (See Figure 20.1 for a sample letter.) It lets the tenants officially know that the building has changed hands, that you are the new owner and that you will be contacting them soon. I suggest you write the letter yourself and have the old landlord sign it. Then you can mail the letter to the tenants. (If you leave this task to the old landlord, it may never get done.)

Figure 20.2 provides a sample new landlord's letter. You should include the following information in this letter:

FIGURE 20.1 Sample Old Landlord's Letter

Date:_____

Tenant's Name:_____

Address:_____

_____

Dear Tenant:

This will serve to inform you that I have sold the property you are currently renting. The anticipated date of title transfer is _____. Please contact the new landlord/owner for needed repairs after that date. Until then, you may continue to reach me at _____.
(phone)

I will be transferring your security/cleaning deposit in the amount of $_____ to the new landlord/owner, who will be responsible for refunding it to you upon move-out, assuming you fulfill your rental agreement obligations. If you have questions about this, please contact the new landlord/owner immediately.

The new landlord/owner is _____, who can be reached at _____, _____.
(address)   *(phone)*

Sincerely,

_____
    (old landlord)

FIGURE 20.2 Sample New Landlord's Letter

Date:_____

Tenant's name:_____

Address:_____

_____

Dear Tenant:

As you may already know, I have purchased the property you are renting. I am writing to you by way of introduction so that you will know who I am and will have some idea of what to expect in the coming months. (I plan to stop by within the next week or so to introduce myself personally.)

You will need to change where you send your rent payments. Please make your next and all future rent payments to

_____,
(name)

_____.
(address)

Rent can be paid in the form of a personal check, money order or cashier's check. It is payable on the due date and is considered late thereafter. If you will have to be late for any reason, please contact me as soon as possible. Late rent can result in the institution of eviction proceedings.

I'm sure you're wondering about your security/cleaning deposit. I will be responsible for returning it to you. However, to ensure proper credit, could you please do something for me? Fill out the information requested below and forward it, along with a copy of your old rental agreement, to me. (I use a different rental agreement and soon will be forwarding a copy for you.)

If you have any questions or concerns, please don't hesitate to call me. If not, I look forward to meeting with you in the very near future.

Sincerely,

_____
(new landlord)

FIGURE 20.2 Sample New Landlord's Letter (Continued)

Tenants' Questionnaire

Property Address: _____

Tenant's Name: _____

Other Tenant's Name: _____

Number of Adult Occupants:____Names: _____

Number of Children:___Ages: _____

Number of Pets: ___Type: _____

Number of Cars:___Type:_____License #: _____

Type:_____License #: _____

Employer: _____

Phone at Work: _____

Current Rental Rate: $ _____

Date Rent Is Due: _____

Date Rent Currently Paid To: _____

Date Moved In: _____

Date Lease Ends (unless Month-to-Month):_____

Amount of Last Month's Rent Paid: $ _____

Refundable Security Deposit Paid: $ _____

Other Deposits Paid: $ _____

Purpose: _____

Are Any of the Following Appliances or Coverings Your Own Personal Property? [ ]stove [ ]washer [ ]dryer [ ]refrigerator [ ]carpeting [ ]wall coverings [ ]other: _____

Notify in Case of Emergency:_____Phone:_____

Your Phone: _____

Signature: _____

- Introduce yourself.

- Indicate that you have your own rental agreement that you want the tenants to sign.

- Indicate that you are responsible for deposits and last months' rents, and ask the tenants to come forward with copies of their rental agreements, cancelled checks or other evidence of having paid in monies.

- Indicate how you intend to collect the rent in the future.

- Give tenants your correct address and phone number so they know where to send the rent and how to contact you.

Changing Rental Agreements

One thing that you will most certainly want to do is to begin using your own rental agreement with the tenants. However, you cannot simply step in and change rental agreements. You are bound by the agreement signed by the old landlord. If it's a lease, you will have to wait until the lease term is up to change it. You can, however, offer the tenant some incentive—such as reduced rent, a few weeks free or a better apartment—to change it sooner.

With a standard month-to-month agreement, you can usually change the agreement with appropriate notice, often 30 days. However, you will need the tenants to sign your new agreement before it becomes effective.

Sometimes a tenant will refuse to sign your new agreement and insist on staying put under the old landlord's agreement. Perhaps the tenant objects to a clause in your agreement. Your choices are either to change your rental agreement, which you probably won't want to do, or to ask the tenant to move. My suggestion is that if you value the tenant, you play it carefully and compromise as much as possible.

Changes in Rent

When buying a rental property, the buyer often plans to raise rents. After all, the value of such property is normally determined by the amount of income it produces. Raise rents and you've increased your equity, sometimes quite substantially.

If you feel that the market justifies higher rents than are currently being paid by the tenants, I suggest you raise them as soon as possible, preferably within the first three months. (With leases, of course, you will have to wait until the lease term runs out to raise the rent.) The tenants will understand that the rents are being raised as part of the change in ownership and will either accept it or move. If you've checked the market carefully, they'll quickly see that the rents are only being raised to realistic levels, and most will stay. Nevertheless, anytime you raise rents you always run the risk that some tenants will move rather than pay.

A Higher Last Month's Rent

With leases, the tenants probably will have paid the last month's rent in advance. However, you cannot raise the rent during the term of the lease (unless there is a specific clause in the lease allowing this). Furthermore, the total amount of money to be paid over the term is usually specified. Thus, you can't increase the last month's rent for a lessee even though other tenants may be paying more now.

Where this really becomes an issue is with a tenant who originally rented on a lease, stayed past the expiration of the lease and is now on a month-to-month basis. That tenant, through several rent increases, may now be paying $1,000 a month, although he or she originally paid only $750 for the last month's rent. Can you now insist on the extra $250 when the tenant decides to move and the issue of the last month comes up?

It depends on how your original lease was written. But in any event, I can guarantee that the tenant is not going to look with pleasure upon paying that extra $250. In fact, most tenants will fight you tooth and nail over the money.

I suggest you calmly ask the tenant for the money and explain why it's owed to you. However, if the tenant protests strongly, I suggest that either you compromise and accept half or if it's only one tenant, write it off. Sometimes the hassle just isn't worth it. Yes, it's important to be right, but not if you have a heart attack in the process.

Getting Copies of Keys

Ideally, the old landlord was well organized and had a separate set of duplicate keys for each rental unit. In the real world, however, the old landlord may actually have been a complete dud when it came to keeping track of little things like keys. He or she may only have had a master. In a worst-case scenario, the old landlord may not have any keys at all to turn over to you!

Keep in mind that you must have keys to each rental unit you manage. There could be a fire or other emergency requiring you to gain immediate access to the unit. Without a key your only recourse would be to break the door down. Thus, you will have the unpleasant job of asking each tenant for their keys so you can make a duplicate set. If they are hesitant about giving them up, point out why you need the keys and what you would have to do if you didn't get them. I can't think of a single tenant I've known who would rather have his or her door knocked down rather than give up a key. Nevertheless, should a tenant still refuse, you may have to get an attorney to press this issue. You can't compromise; you must have keys to all your rental units.

Getting the Tenants To Sign Your Rental Agreement

You may not have much information on the existing tenants. Therefore, before you have them sign new rental agreements, ask them to fill out an information sheet. You can use the basic rental application form from Chapter 10, although don't insist on all of the financial information. After all, they are already living in the property.

You need to obtain the following information about the existing tenants:

- Their rental term and type of agreement

- The number of tenants as well as names, ages and pets

- Where they work and the type of cars they own

- Who to call in an emergency

- Which personal property (appliances, wall coverings and so on) belongs to them

- How much they have put up in a deposit/last month's rent as evidenced by a rental agreement, canceled checks and so on

---

◆

Landlord's Hint

You can get some information about existing tenants' finances by noting the bank and account number on the check by which they pay and keeping that information for future reference. (But remember, unless they authorize it in writing, you shouldn't do a credit check on them.)

Early in the process, give a copy of your rental agreement to the tenant along with a date by which you want it signed (of course, keeping in mind the limitations previously noted plus any other limitations imposed by local or state ordinance).

Once you have the information on the tenant, you can call, perhaps a week before you want the agreement signed, and ask them if they have any questions or don't understand anything. Finally, make a date to visit the tenant with a copy of the agreement that you have filled out for their signature.

PART FIVE

◆◆◆◆◆◆◆

Resources

21

◆◆◆◆◆◆◆

When To Hire a Property Management Firm

Since this book is about troubleshooting, you may reasonably wonder why a chapter on hiring an outside firm to handle your property management is included. After all, isn't that like admitting you can't really do it yourself?

Yes and no. Sometimes you can get so frustrated that you really can't do it yourself. Rather than get an ulcer, it may be better to throw in the towel.

In this chapter we will also look at rental management from a business perspective. We'll see if it makes not only emotional but financial sense to have someone else manage your rentals for you.

When You Have a Problem Tenant

We've already talked at length about problem tenants and all the troubles they can cause you. Of course, there's always eviction, the ultimate solution. However, sometimes you don't want to evict a problem tenant, particularly one who pays the rent or is in a unit that's particularly difficult to rent up. You may have a tenant you want to keep, although he or she just keeps giving you all sorts of headaches.

◆

A Management Firm Provides the Solution for Sally's Problem Tenants

Sally had a single-family house with a pool that she rented out to a lovely couple with two charming small children. They seemed to be wonderful people who were concerned with their environment, anxious about the condition of the house and eager to get their rent in on time.

But as soon as they moved in, they began complaining. The screen door didn't slide easily. There were ants in the house. Then they found a big spider. The carpets weren't clean enough. The windows didn't lock properly. The pool cleaning person didn't come often enough.

Of course, Sally responded to all of the complaints quickly, but often they were trivial. For example, she called an exterminator for the ants. Then she called him back for the spider. But he explained that he wouldn't guarantee a spiderless house. The only way to keep spiders out was to get rid of all the cobwebs in the corners and elsewhere. Then she called a handyman to work on the windows and the sliding screen door, but he couldn't find a problem.

The tenants did pay their rent on time, and it was an older house in a not-so-wonderful neighborhood, so Sally didn't want to lose them. But their weekly (or more often) calls became extremely annoying. Furthermore, because they talked to her so often, she began to feel they were becoming overly familiar and expected favors. One time they called to tell her their rent would be a week late but were sure she would understand and that they could count on her friendship.

Finally, Sally began to realize that these tenants, though probably not doing so consciously, were getting under her skin and keeping her from being a good landlord. The final straw was when she planned on raising the rent and realized she just couldn't make herself tell them. She had become an ineffective landlord.

So she hired a professional property management firm. They charged her 10 percent of the rental income but raised rents the first month by 10 percent and so quickly paid for their cost. More to the point, they fielded all the complaints effectively and for the first time in a long time, Sally could relax and not dread the phone ringing for fear it was her problem tenants.

As in Sally's case, the outside property management firm plays an important role—that of intermediary. The firm steps in between you and the tenant and gives you some distance. Furthermore, a firm is often better able to deal with the tenant because it can always say, "Well, you know the owner insists that we raise the rent. What can we do? We're just the managers." Just as a real estate agent acts as a kind of referee between buyer and seller, the property management firm can act as a go-between for you and your tenant. It can tell the tenant something unpleasant for them to hear, such as the rent's going up or their dirty house is the reason why they have spiders. And if the tenants get mad, it's usually at the bearer of the bad news, the property management firm, not the owner.

When a tenant becomes too frustrating to deal with or a property is too hard to handle, it may be time to call for outside help. In the long run this will not only make it easier for you to sleep at night, but it may also save you money.

When the Property Is Too Far Away

Another good reason for having a property management firm is when you own property more than an hour or so away from home. Let's face it, for most of us it's a mistake to buy distant rentals. We can't be there to rent them up. We can't easily handle maintenance or repairs. We can't pop right over when the tenant has a crisis. We can't be "Johnny on the spot" when the rent's late. In short, it's difficult to be a good landlord from a distance.

But for a fee, a property management firm can do all of these things for us. It can be our representative right on the spot. But if you don't want to pay the money for a property management firm just because your property is far away, buy rental property close to home.

Landlord's Rule #40

Never buy rental property more than an hour away from your home. Try not to buy property more than half an hour away. If you do buy distant property, use a good property management firm to handle it for you.

Tax Consequences of Using a Property Management Firm

While it's beyond the scope of this book to get into the tax considerations of real estate, some insights into problems associated with property management firms might be useful. Please note that the information that follows is not complete. You should check with your tax specialist for details.

Under the tax code, you may be able to write off up to $25,000 in losses on rental real estate against your regular income (provided you meet certain requirements, one of which is that your regular income be below $100,000 to get the full write-off and below $150,000 to get a partial write-off). However, one of the conditions is that you must actively participate in the management of your rental property.

Hiring a property management firm, however, doesn't mean you aren't actively participating. You may still be able to get the write-off, provided you actively make the important decisions, such as to whom to rent, whom to evict, what rental form to use and so forth. Thus, using a property management firm does not, by itself, mean that you won't be able to get a write-off on your rentals.

As noted, this is a complex subject, and you should check with your tax specialist for the details. I also suggest my new book with tax attorney Norman Lane, *Tips and Traps for Saving on All of Your Real Estate Taxes* (McGraw-Hill, 1994), or *The Real Estate Investor's Tax Guide*, by Vernon Hoven (Real Estate Education Company, 1993).

22

♦♦♦◆♦♦♦

Keeping Good Records

You need to keep good records for at least two reasons. The first is that you need to know who paid you what and when so that you won't charge someone twice, as well as which bills you've paid so you won't pay them a second time. The second reason is the IRS. The IRS requires that you keep documentation for all income and expenses so that you can substantiate them, if called upon to do so. The last thing you want is for the government to deny your deductions because you can't come up with invoices and receipts.

The Paper Way

If you own one or even a handful of rental units, you don't need a fancy system for keeping records. You can buy a filing box with separators in it and make divisions for each property and even headings under different properties (see Figure 22.1). Within each property division, you can keep a separate folder for electrical repairs, plumbing repairs, pool maintenance, gardening and so forth. For example, you'll have a division for the Rover Street house with half a dozen folders in it as well as a division for the Adams Crest rental with folders in it and so on. As you pay each bill, you put the invoice in the appropriate folder, noting the check number and date you paid it.

FIGURE 22.1   Paper Filing System

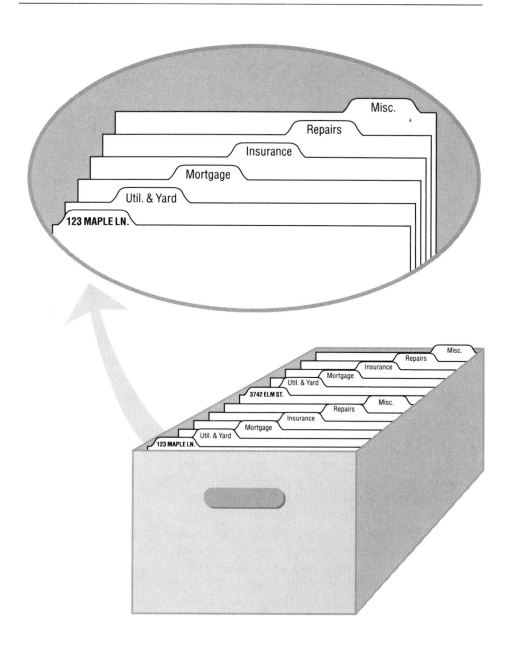

As bills come in, they can all be kept in a separate folder marked "to be paid." Put new bills into the back and pay from the front, and you'll always be paying your oldest bills first.

And you can keep a ledger into which you record all monies received, from whom, the date and the purpose. Many accountants advise that you place all income from your rentals into a single account that is separate from your personal account to avoid confusion and the chance that someone will later say you failed to properly record rental income.

Armed with your file of documented expenses, your income ledger and your checkbook (and monthly statements and returned checks), you should be able to withstand an audit and keep track of all your monies coming in and going out.

Rent and Expense Schedules

If you have only one rental unit, this really isn't important. You can always keep track of who has paid and when in your general ledger.

However, as you add rental units, it becomes increasingly difficult to remember what the money paid was for, who paid it and so on. Therefore, a rental income schedule with the names of tenants and their addresses, the date and amount they paid and the purpose (laundry money income is different from rental money income) is helpful. It will let you know at a glance what money has come in, from where and for what purpose. (See Figure 22.2 for a sample rental schedule.)

Similarly, a rental expense schedule showing each unit separately and the expenses paid monthly, such as mortgage, utilities, maintenance and so forth, will help you keep track of where your money is going from moment to moment.

Depreciation

One expense that no landlord/owner wants to forget is depreciation on their building (not their land). The amount you can deduct for depreciation varies depending on when you put the property into service and the type of property involved. Furthermore, although adding depreciation into your expense/income calculations can turn a profitable property into a losing proposition (at least on paper), it

---

FIGURE 22.2   Tenant Rental Schedule

Page 1—Tenant Records

TENANT #1

TENANT NAME: _____

TENANT ADDRESS: _____

TENANT PHONE: _____

RENTAL RATE: $ _____

DEPOSITS HELD: $ _____

MOVED IN: _____

TENANT #2

TENANT NAME: _____

TENANT ADDRESS: _____

TENANT PHONE: _____

RENTAL RATE: $ _____

DEPOSITS HELD: $ _____

MOVED IN: _____

TENANT #3

TENANT NAME: _____

TENANT ADDRESS: _____

TENANT PHONE: _____

RENTAL RATE: $ _____

DEPOSITS HELD: $ _____

MOVED IN: _____

FIGURE 22.2 (Continued)

TENANT #4

TENANT NAME: _____

TENANT ADDRESS: _____

TENANT PHONE: _____

RENTAL RATE: $ _____

DEPOSITS HELD: $ _____

MOVED IN: _____

TENANT #5

TENANT NAME: _____

TENANT ADDRESS: _____

TENANT PHONE: _____

RENTAL RATE: $ _____

DEPOSITS HELD: $ _____

MOVED IN: _____

TENANT #6

TENANT NAME: _____

TENANT ADDRESS: _____

TENANT PHONE: _____

RENTAL RATE: $ _____

DEPOSITS HELD: $ _____

MOVED IN: _____

FIGURE 22.2   Tenant Rental Schedule (Continued)

Page 2—Rental Schedule

Tenant #	JAN	FEB	MAR	Month APRIL	MAY	JUNE
1	$	$	$	$	$	$
2	$	$	$	$	$	$
3	$	$	$	$	$	$
4	$	$	$	$	$	$
5	$	$	$	$	$	$
6	$	$	$	$	$	$
Totals						

---

doesn't mean you can necessarily write off the loss in the current year. The active/passive rules of the 1986 Tax Reform Act may prevent you from writing off any loss on your real estate in the current year, although you will be able to carry it forward (new rules in 1993 allow special exceptions for real estate professionals). Check with your tax specialist. I also recommend *Tips and Traps for Saving on All of Your Real Estate Taxes* (McGraw-Hill, 1994), by Irwin and Lane, for more information on this complex subject.

In any event, it's a good idea to keep track of your depreciation so that you can see at a glance where you stand on any property. Create a separate expense folder for depreciation by property and record it annually.

Computerizing

Of course, in this day of home computers it's somewhat like being in the Dark Ages not to have a program that does all these rental and expense calculations for you and much more. Even simple programs available for under $50 will allow you to put entries into rent and expense schedules. Indeed, they will do much more, including keep all entries on track in a general ledger as well as provide monthly operating statements and annual statements that even indicate which items are tax-deductible and which aren't. (In a rental situation, almost everything eventually should be tax-deductible.)

Furthermore, a good computer program can generate reports that can provide you with much useful information, such as your monthly maintenance costs, your monthly mortgage expense, your insurance costs, utility costs and so on. It can even let you know when one of your units is generating unusually high expenses.

Landlord's Rule #41

Get everything written on paper—every expense, every bit of income. Never trust your memory—no one else will.

APPENDIXES

•••◆•••

Appendix A
Rental Agreement

Appendix B
Walk-Through Inspection Sheets

Appendix C
Landlord's Rules

CAVEAT *Portions of the following rental agreement may not apply to your circumstances or may not be legal in your state or area.* **Do not use it or any prewritten document as it is.** *Take it to a competent attorney in your area so that it may be customized for your state and locale and for your particular needs. The author and publisher assume no responsibility for the legality, appropriateness or timeliness of this agreement.*

TENANCY AGREEMENT
MONTH-TO-MONTH/LEASE

THIS DOCUMENT IS INTENDED TO BE A LEGALLY BINDING AGREEMENT. READ IT CAREFULLY.

City: _____

State: _____

Date: _____

_____, hereinafter referred to as landlord, agrees to rent to _____, hereinafter referred to as tenants, the property described as _____, hereinafter referred to as the premises, together with the following personal property: carpets, window coverings, light fixtures, built-in appliances, plus the following furniture:

_____

_____

Cross out and initial one of the two following paragraphs that does not apply, and fill out and initial the one that does.

[ ] LEASE This tenancy shall commence on _____19__ and terminate on _____19__. The total rent for this lease period is $_____. The tenants shall pay first and last month's rent in advance. Upon expiration of this agreement, the tenancy shall revert to a month-to-month tenancy at $_____ per month.

[ ] MONTH-TO-MONTH This tenancy shall commence on _____19__ and may be terminated by either party by giving a 30-day WRITTEN notice of termination to the other party.

1. RENT The rent is $_____ per month, payable in advance on the ____day of each calendar month. Tenants to pay rent at the office of the landlord at_____, (*city*) _____, (*state*) _____, (*ZIP*) _____ or at such other place as the landlord may from time to time designate.

2. BAD CHECKS Tenants shall pay a $_____ charge for handling of each check returned by the tenants' bank for "insufficient funds." Any dishonored check shall be treated as unpaid rent. It is hereby mutually agreed that if the tenants' bank returns two checks for whatever reason, thereafter tenants shall pay all rent in the form of cash, cashier's check or money order. Any rent not received by the fifth day after it is due shall be paid only in the form of cash, cashier's check or money order.

3. SECURITY DEPOSIT

UNDER NO CIRCUMSTANCES SHALL THE SECURITY DEPOSIT BE USED AS THE LAST MONTH'S RENT.

Tenants agree to pay a refundable security deposit of $_____ before occupying the premises. Said deposit shall be refunded within ____days along with a written accounting of disposition of said deposit after tenants completely vacate the premises provided:

A. No damage, other than normal wear and tear, has been done to the premises, the furniture or other personal property.
B. Premises are left clean. Landlord may deduct a portion of deposit to pay for certain cleaning if premises are not left clean.
C. All utilities that are the tenants' responsibility have been paid for in full, and utilities have been properly notified of the tenants' departure.
D. All keys have been returned to the landlord.
E. All other conditions and terms of this agreement have been satisfactorily fulfilled.

The landlord may use all or a portion of this security deposit as may be reasonably necessary to:

A. remedy tenants' defaults in payment of rent;
B. clean premises if left uncleaned by tenants; and
C. repair damages caused by tenants to premises.

If any portion of the security deposit is used during the term of the tenancy to cure a default in rent or to repair damages, tenants agree to reinstate security deposit to its full amount within _____ days of written notice delivered to tenants by landlord in person or by mail.

In addition to the above, tenants also agree to pay a refundable pet security deposit of $_____.

In addition to the above, tenants also agree to pay a refundable waterbed deposit of $_____.

In addition to the above, tenants also agree to pay a NONREFUNDABLE cleaning fee of $_____.

4. LATE FEE It is hereby agreed that if the rent is not paid by the date it is due, tenants shall pay a late fee of $_____ for each day from the rental due date until the rent is paid.

5. INSPECTION Prior to taking occupancy, tenants agree to inspect the premises and any personal property therein and to execute an inspection sheet which shall become a part of this agreement.

6. ACCESS Tenants shall allow the landlord access to the premises at reasonable times and upon reasonable notice for the purposes of inspection, making necessary repairs or showing the premises to prospective tenants or purchasers.

7. NOTICE If rent is not paid by the due date, landlord may serve tenants with a _____ day notice to pay rent. If landlord agrees to accept payment of rent in full and late fees after serving notice, tenants shall in addition be subject to a $_____ fee for preparing and serving the notice.

8. OCCUPANCY The total number of people who may occupy the premises is _____. The names and birthdays of children (under age 18) who will occupy the premises are:

_____

_____

_____

No pet (except an animal trained to serve the handicapped, such as a Seeing Eye dog) shall be kept on the premises without the specific written permission of the owner. The following pet(s) may be kept: _____.

9. VEHICLES Landlord shall provide ___ covered and ___ uncovered parking areas for tenants. Tenants shall keep a maximum of _____ vehicles on the premises. All tenants' vehicles not kept in designated locations must be parked in public areas. Tenants shall park no boat, trailer or recreational vehicle on the

premises continuously for more than ___ days without prior written approval of the landlord.

10. DAMAGES AND REPAIRS Tenants agree to pay for all damages to the premises done by the tenants or their invitees. Tenants agree not to paint, paper, alter, redecorate or make repairs to the dwelling, except as provided by law, without first obtaining the landlord's specific written permission.

Landlord agrees to undertake as soon as possible any and all repairs necessary to make the premises habitable and to correct any defects that are hazardous to the health and safety of the occupants, upon notification by tenants of the problem. If the landlord cannot reasonably complete such repairs within three days, he (she) shall keep tenants informed of the work progress.

All requests by tenants for service and repairs, except in the case of an emergency, are to be in the form of writing. Tenants agree to keep the premises in good order and condition and to pay for any repairs caused by their negligence or misuse or that of their family or invitees.

It is mutually agreed that it is the tenants' responsibility to repair certain items, such as windows broken or damaged subsequent to tenants' occupancy, at tenants' expense. If tenants are unable or unwilling to repair broken or damaged windows within a reasonable period of time, landlord may make such repairs and charge tenants. The cost of the repairs must not exceed the lowest bid by a competent workman.

As of occupancy, landlord warrants that all plumbing drainage is in good working condition. Tenants thereafter agree to pay for removing all stoppages caused for any reason except for roots, defective plumbing, backup from main lines or undefined causes as determined by the plumber who clears the line.

11. USE The premises are to be used only as a residence. No commercial use is allowed. The tenants shall have the right to quiet enjoyment of the premises. The tenants agree not to disturb, annoy, endanger or inconvenience neighbors nor use the premises for any immoral or unlawful purpose, nor violate any law ordinance nor commit waste or nuisance upon or about the premises. No waterbed may be used on the premises without the prior written consent of the landlord.

12. UTILITIES Landlord shall pay for the following utilities:

_____.

Tenants shall be responsible for opening, closing and paying all costs for the following utilities: _____

_____.

If the tenants are responsible for trash, the tenants shall obtain and maintain trash and garbage service from the appropriate utility company.

13. YARD MAINTENANCE Landlord shall be responsible for maintaining all common areas. Tenants shall be responsible for maintaining

_____.

With regard to areas tenants are to maintain, they shall be kept clear of rubbish and weeds. Lawns, shrubs and surrounding grounds shall be kept in reasonably good condition. In the event tenants do not maintain premises in reasonably good condition, landlord at his option may provide gardening service at $____ per month to be paid for by tenants. Landlord shall be responsible for installation, repair and replacement of all below-ground sprinkler systems.

14. INSURANCE The landlord shall obtain fire insurance to cover the premises. Tenants are aware that landlord's insurance does not cover tenants' personal property, and they are encouraged to secure a tenants' insurance policy.

In the event of fire or casualty damage caused by tenants, they shall be responsible for payment of rent and for repairs to correct the damage. If a portion of the premises should become uninhabitable due to fire or casualty damage due to no fault of the tenants, they shall not be responsible for payment of rent for that portion. Should the entire premises be uninhabitable due to no fault of the tenants, no rent shall be due until premises shall be made habitable again. The landlord shall reserve the right to determine whether premises or a portion thereof is uninhabitable.

15. HAZARDOUS MATERIALS Tenants agree not to keep or use on the premises any materials which an insurance company may deem hazardous or to conduct any activity which increases the rate of insurance for the landlord.

16. NEGLIGENCE Tenants agree to hold the landlord harmless from claims of loss or damage to property and injury or death to persons caused by the negligence or intentional acts of the tenants or their invitees.

17. EMERGENCIES In the event of an emergency involving the premises, such as a plumbing stoppage, the tenants shall immediately call the landlord at _____, or other phone number as the landlord may from time to time designate, and report problem.

18. DELAY If the landlord shall be unable to give possession of the premises on the day of the commencement of this agreement by reason of the holding over of any prior occupant of the premises or for any other reasons beyond the control of the landlord, then tenants' obligations to pay the rent and other charges in this agreement shall not commence until possession of the premises is given or is available to tenants. Tenants agree to accept such abatement of

rent as liquidated damages in full satisfaction of the failure of landlord to give possession of said premises on agreed date and further agree that landlord shall not be held liable for any damages tenants may suffer as a consequence of not receiving timely possession.

19. SUBLETTING Tenants shall not sublet, assign or transfer all or part of the premises without the prior written consent of the landlord.

20. RULES Tenants shall comply with all covenants, conditions and restrictions that apply to the premises. The tenants shall comply with all rules of a homeowners' association that apply to the premises.

21. ATTORNEY'S FEES If either party brings action to enforce any terms of this agreement or recover the possession of the premises, the prevailing party shall/shall not (*cross out wording not desired and initial change*) be entitled to recover from the other party his or her costs and attorney fees.

22. RESPONSIBILITY TO PAY RENT All undersigned tenants are jointly and severally (together and separately) liable for all rents incurred during the term of this agreement. (Every member is equally responsible for the payment of the rent.) Each tenant who signs this agreement authorizes and agrees to be the agent of all other occupants of the premises and agrees to accept, on behalf of the other occupants, service of notices and summons relating to tenancy.

23. SUBSTITUTION OF TENANTS In the event one tenant moves out and is substituted by another, the new tenant shall fill out an application and tenancy shall be subject to the approval of the landlord. No portion of the cleaning deposit will be refunded until the property is completely vacated.

24. HOLD OVER If after the date of termination of tenancy, tenants are still in possession of premises, they will be considered holding over and agree to pay rental damages at the rate of 1/30th of their then current monthly rent per day of holdover.

25. OTHER CONDITIONS Each provision herein containing words used in the singular shall include the plural where the context requires. If any item in this agreement is found to be contrary to federal, state or local law, it shall be considered null and void and shall not affect the validity of any other item in the agreement. The waiver of any breach of any of the terms and conditions of this lease shall not constitute a continuing waiver or a subsequent breach of any of the terms or conditions herein. The foregoing constitutes the entire agreement between the parties and may be nullified or changed only in writing and signed by both parties. Both parties have executed this lease in duplicate and hereby acknowledge receipt of a copy on the day and year first shown above. Time is the essence of this agreement.

TENANTS ACKNOWLEDGE RECEIPT OF THE FOLLOWING:

[ ] Move-in inspection sheet

[ ] Homeowners' rules and regulations

[ ] Entry key

[ ] Community pool key

[ ] Remote garage door opener

[ ] Security gate card #_____

[ ] Laundry room key

[ ] Other: _____

Tenant: _____

Tenant: _____

Landlord: _____

Landlord: _____

WALK-THROUGH INSPECTION SHEETS

Date: _____

Property Address: _____

Tenant's Names: _____

Tenant's Names: _____

Landlord's Name: _____

LIVING ROOM, DINING ROOM, FAMILY ROOM, LOFT, BREAKFAST ROOM
(Use separate sheet for each room.)

Item	Condition on Arrival	Condition on Departing
		Tenants responsible for damage beyond normal wear and tear and for areas not cleaned.
Floor Coverings		
Walls and Ceiling		
Light Fixtures		
Windows and Screens		
Window Rods and Coverings		
Doors (including hardware)		
Slider and Screen Door		
Fireplace and Equipment		
Other:		

Date: _____

Signed by landlord: _____

Signed by tenant: _____

KITCHEN

Item	Condition on Arrival	Condition on Departing
		Tenants responsible for damage beyond normal wear and tear and for areas not cleaned.
Floor Coverings		
Cupboards		
Walls and Ceilings		
Windows and Screens		
Window/Slider Coverings		
Doors, including hardware		
Light Fixtures		
Counter Surfaces and Makeup		
Sink Faucets		
Garbage Disposal		
Stove Burners		
Fan		

Item	Condition on Arrival	Condition on Departing
Stove Light		
Clock		
Oven Heating Elements		
Broiler		
Light		
Sink Drain		
Dishwasher		
Other:		

Date: _____

Signed by landlord: _____

Signed by tenant: _____

BATHROOM

Item	Condition on Arrival	Condition on Departing
		Tenants responsible for damage beyond normal wear and tear and for areas not cleaned.
Floor Covering		
Walls and Ceiling		
Shower and Tub (doors, tracks)		

Item	Condition on Arrival	Condition on Departing
Toilet		
Plumbing Fixtures		
Windows and Screens		
Doors and Hardware		
Light Fixtures		
Sink and Counter		
Fan		
Misc.:		

Date: _____

Signed by landlord: _____

Signed by tenant: _____

BEDROOM
(Use separate sheet for each bedroom.)

Item	Condition on Arrival	Condition on Departing
		Tenants responsible for damage beyond normal wear and tear and for areas not cleaned.
Floor Covering		
Walls and Ceiling		
Closet, Doors and Track		

Item	Condition on Arrival	Condition on Departing
Windows and Screens		
Window Coverings		
Doors and Hardware		
Light Fixtures		
Fireplace and Equipment		
Gas Valve		
Misc.:		

Date: _____

Signed by landlord: _____

Signed by tenant: _____

HALLWAY AND ENTRYWAY

Item	Condition on Arrival	Condition on Departing
		Tenants responsible for damage beyond normal wear and tear and for areas not cleaned.
Floor Coverings		
Walls and Ceiling		
Closet Doors		
Light Fixtures		

Item	Condition on Arrival	Condition on Departing
Air Conditioning and Heating Filters		
Smoke Alarms		
Other:		

UTILITY ROOM

Item	Condition on Arrival	Condition on Departing
		Tenants responsible for damage beyond normal wear and tear and for areas not cleaned.
Floor Covering		
Walls and Ceiling		
Light Fixtures		
Gas or Electric Service		
Other:		

Date: _____

Signed by landlord: _____

Signed by tenant: _____

GARAGE

Item	Condition on Arrival	Condition on Departing
		Tenants responsible for damage beyond normal wear and tear and for areas not cleaned.
Washer Faucet		
Washer Drain		
Water Softener		
Furnace and Filter		
Air Conditioner		
Light Fixtures		
Floor Type and Condition		
Tools and Equipment		

Date: _____

Signed by landlord: _____

Signed by tenant: _____

YARD

Item	Condition on Arrival	Condition on Departing
	FRONT	*Tenants responsible for damage beyond normal wear and tear and for areas not cleaned.*
Sprinklers		

Item	Condition on Arrival	Condition on Departing
Water Bibs		
Lawn		
Entry Light		
Walkway and Driveway		
Wall/Fence		
Garage Door		
Door Opener (includes remotes)		
Entry Door		
Door Bell		
Other:		

Item	Condition on Arrival	Condition on Departing
	SIDE	*Tenants responsible for damage beyond normal wear and tear and for areas not cleaned.*
Sprinklers		
Water Bibs		

Item	Condition on Arrival	Condition on Departing
Lawn		
Light Fixture		
Walkway		
Wall/Fence		
Door		
Other:		

Item	Condition on Arrival	Condition on Departing
	REAR	*Tenants responsible for damage beyond normal wear and tear and for areas not cleaned.*
Sprinklers		
Water Bibs		
Lawn		
Light Fixture		
Walkway		
Wall/Fence		
Door		

Item	Condition on Arrival	Condition on Departing
Patio		
Patio Cover		
Other:		

Date: _____

Signed by landlord: _____

Signed by tenant: _____

LANDLORD'S RULES

1. Go into the corner and say three times, "I will do *nothing* until I hear what the tenant has to say."

2. Never own rental property in an area in which you are personally afraid to go and pick up the rent.

3. Be a "no nonsense" landlord, but do *not* be mean, vindictive, loud, insulting or overbearing. Always speak quietly and calmly, but firmly. The rent is due. You're there to pick it up. There are no excuses.

4. The rent must always be paid first.

5. Always be soft-spoken and polite; never be seen as an aggressive person or as one who is out of control.

6. Whatever you give away in favors to the tenant, you probably will never get back.

7. There are no acceptable excuses for late rent.

8. Don't let the tenant paint the property.

9. Never let the tenants make improvements or alterations to the property.

10. Never ignore tenants' requests for repairs involving habitability to the property. Always handle them promptly yourself.

11. Always be friendly with your tenants; never be their friends.

12. Never ask the tenants to take on more maintenance than they can handle.

13. Never give rent deductions. For example, don't reduce the rent by $30 if the tenant waters the yard properly. Almost immediately the tenant will think of the rental rate as $30 less and will forget about what has to be done to earn that money. On the other hand, if you send a check *made payable to the water company* for $30 each month (e.g., so that the lawns are mowed and shrubs trimmed), you have a continuing incentive that is tied directly to the maintenance task you want accomplished. (Note: don't write the check to the tenant or you could fall under federal or state employer rules.)

14. Don't insist that your tenants follow your lifestyle or your family rules. You will only become ineffectual and frustrated.

15. Always try to rent your properties from the 1st to the 1st. (Most tenants are available to move in on the 1st. If you try to rent from the 15th, they

will want the rent to start on the 1st anyway and you could lose two weeks payment.)

16. Less is more when it comes to classified advertising.

17. Always emphasize tenant benefits when you're trying to rent up your property.

18. No tenant is better than having a bad tenant.

19. When a prospective tenant calls, the aim of your conversation should always be to get the tenant to the property. You can't sign a rental agreement over the phone.

20. A clean house attracts a clean tenant.

21. Never rent to anyone who doesn't fill out an application. Never rent before checking out the application. Do a good job when you check out the tenant.

22. Get the cash.

23. A lease locks in only those who have some assets and who want to be locked in.

24. Never allow a tenant into a property until you have received *all* the deposits.

25. Never let the tenant move in until you have the *cash.* After all, what if you take their personal check to their bank and find that they don't have sufficient funds to cover it?

26. You always have to pay close attention to your properties, especially when tenants are moving in, are moving out and are in-between.

27. Always paint and clean your rental thoroughly before the tenants move in. That way you'll be able to write down a clean bill of health on the move-in walk-through inspection sheet, which will provide you with the evidence you need to collect for damages when you conduct the move-out walk-through inspection.

28. Allowing the tenant who did the damage to correct it after they move out is like giving an award to the person who helps put out the fire in your barn, after they first set it.

29. If you have a tenant evicted, the chances are almost certain that the property will be left trashed.

30. In the long run, a landlord who's pragmatic will make far more money and avoid many more headaches than a landlord who always insists on being right.

31. The best way to avoid evicting a tenant is not to rent to him or her in the first place. Nothing takes the place of proper screening of tenants.

32. Never, never resort to a self-help eviction of any kind.

33. You can't always rent for what you need to make your monthly payments. But you can always rent for what the market will bear.

34. It's a lot worse to have a property vacant than to have it rented full-time at a lower rate than you want.

35. Don't overlook the inertia factor. Most people don't like to move. It's a hassle. The kids might have to change schools. As a result, your tenants may stay simply because it's easier than moving. Of course, increase the rents high enough and you'll drive any tenant out.

36. The only way to guarantee that you won't need insurance coverage is to carry it.

37. When they move in, always tell your tenants that their belongings are *not* covered under your insurance policy. Encourage them to get their own tenant's policy.

38. Try to avoid converting your residence to a rental if it has a pool, is old and run down, is far off the beaten track or has a high-maintenance yard. If you do convert with these negative features, you may end up with a substantial negative cash flow on the property.

39. When converting isn't advisable, try selling the property or taking in an equity-sharing partner.

40. Never buy rental property more than an hour away from your home. Try not to buy property more than half an hour away. If you do buy distant property, use a good property management firm to handle it for you.

41. Get everything written on paper—every expense, every bit of income. Never trust your memory—no one else will.

Index